Laura Ingalls Wilder's Little Town

Laura Ingalls Wilder's Little Town
Where History and Literature Meet

JOHN E. MILLER

 UNIVERSITY PRESS OF KANSAS

© 1994 by the University Press of Kansas

Published by the University Press of Kansas (Lawrence, Kansas 66049),
which was organized by the Kansas Board of Regents and is operated and
funded by Emporia State University, Fort Hays State University, Kansas
State University, Pittsburg State University, the University of Kansas, and
Wichita State University

Library of Congress Cataloging-in-Publication Data

Miller, John E., 1945–
    Laura Ingalls Wilder's little town : where history and literature
meet / John E. Miller.
        p.   cm.
    Includes index.
    ISBN 0-7006-0654-8
    1. Wilder, Laura Ingalls, 1867–1957—Homes and haunts—South
Dakota—De Smet.   2. Wilder, Laura Ingalls, 1867–1957—Criticism and
interpretation.   3. Historical fiction, American—History and
criticism.   4. Children's stories, American—History and criticism.
5. Frontier and pioneer life in literature.   6. Literature and
history—South Dakota.   7. City and town life in literature.   8. De
Smet (S.D.)—In literature.   I. Title.   II. Title: Little town.
PS3545.I342Z77   1994
813'.52—dc20   93-40632

British Library Cataloguing in Publication Data is available.

Printed in the United States of America
10 9 8 7 6 5 4 3 2

For Kathy

Contents

Illustrations

Acknowledgments

Many individuals graciously assisted me with advice, information, suggestions, and illustrations. Dwight Miller at the Herbert Hoover Presidential Library, which holds the Rose Wilder Lane papers, provided many helpful suggestions, and I want to thank Roger L. MacBride for permission to use quotations and information from the Lane papers in this book. Thanks also goes out to librarians and archivists at the State Historical Society of Missouri, which houses the Laura Ingalls Wilder papers; the Detroit Public Library, for the use of two of Wilder's novel manuscripts and other documents; and the Pomona (California) Public Library, for the use of one of the novel manuscripts. Vivian Glover and others at the Laura Ingalls Wilder Society in De Smet, South Dakota, were always cooperative and helpful. I especially want to acknowledge the helpfulness of all the employees at the South Dakota State Historical Society who assisted in locating information and illustrations. Jo Ann Gray was also very helpful at the Laura Ingalls Wilder–Rose Wilder Lane Home and Museum in Mansfield, Missouri, and helped locate illustrations for me.

William T. Anderson provided much helpful advice and also feedback on parts of the manuscript, and I also appreciate Debbie Hanson's comments on several chapters. Also to my editors at the University Press of Kansas, who did much to enhance the manuscript and reduce its infelicities, many thanks. Research grants from the South Dakota Humanities Council and the Herbert Hoover Presidential Library Association helped defray the costs of research, and sabbatical assistance from South Dakota State University provided time to complete the manuscript. To the many others who helped in a variety of ways I am deeply grateful. Finally, to my wife, Kathy, and children, Ann and Tom, thanks for putting up with me and my ''second family.''

1 / Introduction: At the Intersection of History and Literature

This book on Laura Ingalls Wilder and her popular series of children's novels springs from the premise that history and literature are closely intertwined and that each has much to contribute to the other. The reader of literature will understand it better and enjoy it more by placing it in historical context. In like manner, the student of history can learn much about past people, places, and actions by viewing them in the light of imaginative literature that dramatizes them and illuminates the contexts in which they occurred.

As a working historian, I find pleasure, as well as instruction, in reading good fiction set in the historical past. Historians are constrained by fact and must rely upon traces of past events, but the fiction writer possesses creative license to imagine characters, settings, and events and to develop them in myriad ways, so long as they remain within the limits of plausibility. Both must perform an interpretive task. "The historian and the literary artist," Russel B. Nye reminds us, "are bound by the same risks, related by the same liabilities, dependent on the same creative, imaginative powers."[1] The result in both instances is truth, and each version is valid within its own distinctive domain. Historical truth and literary truth are not opposed to each other; rather, they are complementary. We all would be much poorer without being able to call upon them both, since each can correct, support, and amplify the other.

The assumption operating here is that "something happened'' and that it is within the province of both history and literature to discover what that something was. Admitting that the traces of the past are often nebulous, contradictory, and difficult to interpret and recognizing that our knowledge of history is only approximate and open to debate, I stand with those who assert the importance of the quest and the value of its results. Commenting in 1983 upon theories that deny to literature any connection to external reality, René Wellek asserted, "If literature has nothing to say about our minds and the cosmos, about love and death, about humanity in other times and other countries, literature loses its meaning."[2] Likewise, this study assumes that literature refers to human history and accepts that the purpose of both literature and history is to look for significance and meaning in human action.

My coming to the novels of Laura Ingalls Wilder no doubt resembles the way many others have approached them: my wife and I used to read them to our daughter. With De Smet situated only forty miles down the road from our home in Brookings, South Dakota, we were able to visit the Wilder sites several times and to attend the pageant performed there by townspeople in the summer. De Smet was also one of several towns involved in a humanities outreach program sponsored by South Dakota State University. One of our activities was to interview people in De Smet and Lake Preston (eight miles east on Highway 14) and to put together a half-hour radio program on the history of each community. Our family also visited Laura and Almanzo's Rocky Ridge Farm when I returned to Monett, Missouri, for a high school class reunion— Monett, it turns out, lies seventy-five miles west of Mansfield on Highway 60. Fate, it seems, destined a deep involvement for me with Laura Ingalls Wilder.

When I came across an 1883 bird's-eye drawing of De Smet and a map published in the De Smet *Leader* that same year showing the locations of stores and homes in the town, I decided to write an article on place and community in Laura Ingalls Wilder's little town on the prairie. Rereading the Wilder novels set in De Smet for that project suggested other possibilities for research, and working on an article on freedom and control in Wilder's writings led me to consider writing on a series of topics centering around the relationship of history and literature in her novels. This book is the result of that process.

The chapters included in this book are exploratory and not intended to provide a comprehensive interpretation of Laura Ingalls Wilder's work, but they touch on many themes that I consider to be central to it. Running through all of them is the question of the relationship between history and literature. My intention is to illustrate how history nourishes literature and how literature, in turn, informs us about history.

In the process of writing her novels, Wilder discovered that she was also writing history.[3] They shed light on what Lionel Trilling said novels are designed to illuminate: "the look and feel of things, how things are done and what things are worth and what they cost and what the odds are." The novel, Trilling asserted, "is a perpetual quest for reality, the field of its research being always the social world."[4] It is that social reality and Wilder's way of seeing it and depicting it that constitute the primary focus of this book.

The immediate and continuing success of Wilder's novels stems largely from the assumption made by their readers that they are historical—that the stories they relate reconstruct the way things actually were when Laura was a girl. Of course their accessible style—including their vivid descriptions, evocative language, concrete particulars, believable dialogue, and emotional resonance—also contribute to their popularity. Content and form blend in the novels to produce a nostalgic and compelling, yet also nuanced and seemingly realistic, picture of family life on the agricultural frontier toward the end of the nineteenth century.

The careful attention to detail that Wilder and her daughter, Rose Wilder Lane, practiced in their writing enhances the value of the novels as documents for social history. Food preparation and the customs surrounding it are

Laura Ingalls Wilder at age twenty-four. *(Courtesy South Dakota State Historical society)*

featured prominently in many of the books, and readers also learn something about home furnishings, building styles, clothing fashions, work habits, farm economics, methods of travel, town layouts, cultural entertainments, religion, education, and the family.

But before we get carried away with eagerness to read the novels as history, I must issue a note of caution. For one thing, Wilder wrote the first version of her memoirs—

an autobiographical account called "Pioneer Girl"—in 1930 when she was sixty-three years old. The stories she told there and in her subsequent novels were only as accurate and as detailed as her sixty-three-year-old memory would allow. That many of her memories were vivid and authentic we can be sure, but as she herself admitted in letters to her daughter, her recollections were often vague, receding, and sometimes nonexistent. Disentangling what she actually remembered from what she thought or imagined she did poses an almost impossible task. Correspondence with family members and friends and neighbors, reference to relics and keepsakes retained from bygone days, trips back to the scene of the action, and other research helped her nail down some of the facts. The close relationship that exists between the people, places, and activities described in the novels and records that have been preserved in newspapers, courthouse files, maps, photographs, and other sources generates considerable confidence in the general accuracy of Wilder's recollections.

We must recognize, however, the distinction that exists between the novelist's intention and the historian's. Chapter 9 on the opera house and other entertainments in De Smet illustrates that much more was happening in the community than could be described in the books. If the novels constitute a record of the social history of the town—and they certainly do—they are nevertheless stripped-down history, limited in scope because of the vagaries of Wilder's memory, the requirements of narrative technique, and the girlish point of view assumed by the author while she was writing the novels. Each one was told from the point of view of someone the age of Wilder at the time the action was taking place, which meant leaving out whole ranges of activities that otherwise might have been included. In "Pioneer Girl," for example, she related stories about a murderous Kansas clan who buried their victims beneath their house and about a revenge-crazed woman who extorted a farm out of her sister for having had the temerity to marry the man she had wanted to.[5] These episodes were excised when Wilder wrote the novels, which were aimed at children. Subjects of interest to the historian, therefore, often failed to meet her tests of inclusion.

Furthermore, Wilder kept in mind that she was writing fiction, not literal history, although her strict attention to factual accuracy might seem to belie this point. And it is a point that is easily misunderstood or misinterpreted, because the impression mother and daughter gave, and the assumption that book reviewers and readers seemed to take for granted, is that the novels were literal recordings of Laura's life. Scholars have pointed to historical discrepancies and mistakes of fact in the novels; in several of the following chapters I note instances where literary license was practiced. But Wilder always treated the books as if they were actual fact, and her daughter, Rose Wilder Lane, vehemently insisted until her dying day that they were all true—every fact in them. Perhaps Rose wanted to deflect potential criticism from people in and around De Smet who would be quick to detect factual errors in the stories. Perhaps she was merely trying to maintain consistency with previous statements. Perhaps she thought that the legacy of the books—now risen to mythical proportions— would somehow be undermined if it were known that some facts were not literally true. Perhaps her insistence emanated from something more difficult to pin down, a feeling that the books conveyed more than a simple history of the frontier but also embodied timeless truths and principles that somehow would be called into question if any aspect of the books were shown to be false.

Lane did insert some of her own philosophical viewpoint while editing the books for her mother, although one can easily exaggerate the extent of that contribution. A striking example concerns the description of the Fourth of July in 1881. Wilder's draft of that chapter for *Little Town on the Prairie* included only a spare account describing the speech and the reading of the Declaration of Independence at the ceremony in De Smet. Rose greatly expanded the narrative at this point—quoting chunks of

Rose Wilder Lane as a young woman. *(Courtesy Laura Ingalls Wilder–Rose Wilder Lane Museum and Home, Mansfield, Missouri)*

the Declaration, putting words into the mouth of the orator of the day, and, most significantly, having Laura soliloquize about what it means to be free.[6] This episode is probably the starkest instance of Lane's injecting her own philosophy into the books. There was little need for her to insert her own political views into the books, since her mother was also a strong advocate of individual freedom and initiative and skeptical of government intervention in people's lives. But there is no gainsaying that in places Lane did add her own expressions of individualism or emphasize them in her own language.

In enhancing and supplementing history, the novels of Laura Ingalls Wilder simultaneously humanized it, dramatized it, and particularized it. This book concentrates primarily upon the last four novels in the series, set in De Smet, plus a final, posthumously published volume describing what happened during the first four years of her marriage to Almanzo. From the De Smet newspapers that have been preserved, it is possible to cull individual names, places, and happenings that are described in the novels. Many of the types of events that Wilder included in her plots were mentioned in the short local news paragraphs in the De Smet *Leader* during the early 1880s, but the novels contribute a sense of drama, a description of human emotions and feelings, and a delving into individual personality and character that are only intimated in the columns of the local paper. The novels provide a sense of life as lived. They present us with real people, and if every jot and tittle of the stories cannot be assumed to be strictly factual, that fact hardly detracts from the essential human truth they embody.

These are Laura's stories, and readers over the years have not missed that point. The extraordinary popularity of the novels—from the publication of *Little House in the Big Woods* in 1932 until now, and extending as far away as Japan—requires some sort of explanation. The engaging and frequently eloquent style of the books is part of their appeal. Highly descriptive and essentially straightforward—even simple—in their narration, the books at times reach heights of eloquence, especially in their description of the prairie landscape and the huge sky that looms over it. To a considerable degree, Lane deserves credit for editing and polishing the novels and eliminating infelicities of expression and extraneous or obscure detail.

Without her collaboration and expert professional rewriting of the manuscripts, as William Holtz and others have pointed out, the books never would have achieved the popularity and acclaim that they did.[7]

In fact, it is unlikely that the books would ever have been written in the first place or published at all without Lane's continual encouragement to her mother to get going on them, her editorial assistance in their rewriting, and her successful effort to find them a publisher once they were completed. Ironically, had Wilder done a better job with "Pioneer Girl," which Lane tried to peddle to publishers in 1930, its publication probably would have attracted little attention and would no doubt have precluded development of the seven novels that emerged from its story line during the next dozen or so years. That autobiographical manuscript contained the basic outline and many of the details of every novel in the series (except for the second one, *Farmer Boy*, about Almanzo's life). Thus, by failing to be good enough in the beginning, Wilder made it possible to become much better later on.

The key to Wilder's success as a storyteller lies in the dramatic, engaging way in which she transformed the remembered facts of her own life into the materials of imaginative fiction. She was fortunate to have experienced a series of momentous changes as her family traveled hither and yon on the edge of the agricultural frontier during the two decades after the Civil War. Born on February 7, 1867, on a farm near Pepin, Wisconsin, which lay on the Mississippi River, Laura Elizabeth Ingalls was the second of four girls to make up the family of Charles and Caroline Ingalls. The parents' New York and Connecticut roots placed them within the Yankee stream of migration that spread rapidly across the northern part of the Midwest during the nineteenth century.

Of the sisters, only Laura stood out in any way as unusual or possessing special talents, and had she not written her series of children's novels after she turned sixty, she too would have probably been remembered simply as having been a slightly eccentric farm woman who enjoyed involvement in organizations and who had a special way with words (she wrote a regular column for farm newspapers for almost two decades before setting down her childhood experiences in autobiographical form during the 1930s and 1940s). Mary, the oldest sister, was born in 1865 in the Ingalls' cabin near Pepin. The aftereffects of an illness left her blind, which meant that Laura had to look out for her and, in effect, serve as her "eyes" until she went off to a school in Vinton, Iowa. Caroline ("Carrie"), born in Montgomery County, Kansas, in 1870, and Grace, born in 1877 in Burr Oak, Iowa, completed the family. They were Laura's little sisters, whom she enjoyed playing with and for whose care she was also partly responsible. The whole family was griefstricken when the only boy, Charles Frederick ("Freddie") died in 1876 when he was only nine months old.

Lacking capital and often suffering from bad luck, Charles Ingalls, like many of his fellow agriculturalists, found himself frequently scanning the horizon for better opportunities, drawn by reports that life was better just over the horizon. Wherever he went, his family went with him, although his wife, Caroline, anxiously looked forward to the day when her little brood would settle down permanently and call an end to their peripatetic way of life. From Wisconsin, they ventured out to Indian territory in Kansas in 1868; returned to Pepin in 1871; went west to Walnut Grove, Minnesota, in 1874; to Burr Oak, Iowa, in 1876; back to Walnut Grove the following year; and finally out to Dakota Territory in the fall of 1879.

Laura Ingalls Wilder's novels trace her family's wanderings from place to place on the frontier during the time between her first memories as a little girl in Wisconsin until her marriage to Almanzo Wilder, a young homesteader from New York State, in De Smet, Dakota Territory, at the age of eighteen in 1885. The first four years of her marriage were described in an unpublished manuscript that lay undiscovered in a desk drawer until after her daughter Rose Wilder Lane's death. In tracing her family's movements and activities, Wilder was not only telling the story of one frontier family, she was also, in part, chronicling the history of family life on that late-nine-teenth-century frontier.

Out of her rejected "Pioneer Girl" manuscript, Wilder extracted stories about growing up near Pepin, Wisconsin, and expanded them into *Little House in the Big Woods*, which was published by Harper and Row in April 1932. Although Rose edited her mother's prose and further refined it in the process of typing the manuscript for publication, this book, interestingly enough, received less editorial attention from the daughter than did most of the rest. Wilder's prose style by this time was polished enough to stand on its own, for the most part, although several sections received some heavy editing from the daughter.

Perhaps because she had more time on her hands, Rose spent much more time in reworking the next several novels that her mother drafted in pencil in her five-cent, lined tablets. Once having established the routine, Rose continued her heavy-handed editing procedure until the last book in the series, *These Happy Golden Years*, which comes nearest to the first book in standing on its own in the form that the mother had written it. Although Rose's editorial revisions of the books undoubtedly enhanced their charm and readability, the story lines and factual details were essentially the responsibility of the mother. Rose's basic contribution was to modify the language, where she thought doing so would improve it, to elaborate upon scenes that her mother had written, and to tighten the structure of the novels. This work resulted in major rewrites of large parts of books two through seven in the series, but there were long sections in all of the books that needed only slight editorial attention. The process was clearly a collaborative one. Wilder's stories could have stood on their own and achieved popularity, but Rose's contribution certainly enhanced their appeal and helped ensure that they would become classics of children's literature.

The second book in the series, *Farmer Boy* (1933), chronicled Almanzo's childhood days growing up in New York

State. By the time Wilder was drafting it, the response to the first book was so great that she was already looking ahead to extending the series by writing again about her own life. *Little House on the Prairie* (1935) and *On the Banks of Plum Creek* (1937) carried the Ingalls family out to Indian territory in Kansas and back again, and then out to the Minnesota prairie. Their stay in Burr Oak, Iowa, and the death of the only boy to be born to Charles and Caroline Ingalls may have been too sad a time for Wilder to want to include in her story, so she left them out.

By the time the family departed Minnesota for Dakota Territory, Laura was twelve, just entering adolescence, and her powers of observation and social sophistication had advanced considerably beyond what they had been earlier. The last four books in the series, about the Dakota experience, are the primary focus of the following chapters. *By the Shores of Silver Lake* (1939) traced the family's move to the new railroad town of De Smet, as the Chicago and Northwestern Railroad pushed its branch line west of Tracy, Minnesota, in 1879. *The Long Winter* (1940) was a classic story about a quintessential historical episode on the prairie—the deadly, blizzard-filled winter of 1880-1881, which cut off railroad transportation and most travel in eastern Dakota Territory for several months. *Little Town on the Prairie* (1941), more than any other book in the series, chronicled the social history of the small town, as it described Laura's school days in De Smet and her interactions with other children and adults in town. *These Happy Golden Years* (1943) brought the series to an end with Almanzo Wilder's courtship of Laura, their marriage, and their moving to a homestead north of town at the end of the book.

The discovery of another Wilder manuscript after Rose's death led to the publication of *The First Four Years* in 1971. This was obviously the "adult" novel that Wilder had talked about writing during the late 1930s. Much less detailed and less lyrical than the other books, it has been judged less competent and less polished than the others, too. The different tone and stylistic qualities of the book may simply have reflected the facts that Wilder intended it for an adult audience and that Rose's editorial hand was not involved in rewriting it. But also the subject matter—the hardships and tragedies of a young couple starting out in a hostile environment during the late 1880s—undoubtedly altered the tone of this book. Nevertheless, it has much to tell us about the lives that Wilder attempted to describe on the Dakota prairie and will be referred to frequently in the following pages.

The nine chapters that follow are designed to enhance our understanding of and appreciation of Wilder's literary achievement as well as to use the novels as a springboard for deepening our knowledge of the history of the agricultural frontier that encompassed Dakota Territory and the surrounding region during the late nineteenth century. At this intersection of history and literature, I try to use my experience as a historian and my imagination as a reader of literature to carry on an interdisciplinary conversation about one of our most important authors of children's literature. Implicit throughout is the assumption that "children's literature" has much that is worthwhile to say to adults.

Two chapters establish an environmental context for what is to follow. Chapter 2 describes the close connection that existed between place and community in De Smet—"The Little Town on the Prairie"—and suggests how communal relationships emerged out of and were enhanced by the particular settings in which they took place. The next chapter discusses the myriad ways in which two seemingly contradictory notions—freedom and control—were related to each other on the frontier. Control over environmental conditions, economic circumstances, and even other people was often essential if individuals were to realize the kind of freedom they wanted in their lives. Ultimately, in the minds of both Laura Ingalls Wilder and her daughter Rose Wilder Lane, it was self-control that undergirded true freedom. The two concepts thus were, not contradictory, but complementary.

These early chapters establish the general approach that is used in all of the chapters that follow, which is to take two concepts or ideas, such as place and community or freedom and control, and utilize them as spotlights to illuminate old subjects in new ways. My purpose throughout is to investigate Wilder's novels from a variety of angles and thereby to expose some of their meanings in ways that may not have been thought of before. Chapter 4, "Love and Affection in Wilder's Life and Writing," attempts to show how a woman for whom sex and sexuality were distasteful subjects to be avoided could make love and affection central to her life and to her writing. The relationship between the familial love and affection that she experienced during her childhood and the kind of conjugal love that consummated her courtship with Almanzo was a complicated and interesting one.

Chapters 5–7 each deal in some fashion with matters of fact, interpretation, narration, and knowledge. How did Wilder herself come to know the world, how did she represent that world in her writings, and how are we, as readers, to interpret the words she used to describe her experiences? "Fact and Interpretation in Wilder's Fiction" uses Charles Sanders Peirce's semiotic concept of the "interpretant" to ask what kinds of preconceived and inherited ideas, values, and practices helped shape Wilder's thinking in the process of interpreting the world around her. For of all her insistence on the factuality of her books, fictional practices clearly shaped her narratives, and interpretation was integral to her thinking. I deal more with the fictional practices Wilder developed in collaboration with her daughter Rose in Chapter 6, which is about the narrative rules and the storytelling procedures the two relied upon. Stories provided meaning and established identity in people's lives. Storytelling was at the very heart of Wilder's whole way of being, and the stories she told conformed to certain rules of narration, both explicit and implicit. In Chapter 7 the kind of textbook history that Laura Ingalls imbibed as a child is contrasted with the kind of living history she later incorporated in her novels. The entire series, in effect, supplies its readers with a social history of the frontier.

The final three chapters discuss the "real world" that lay beyond the familial environment Laura grew up in and, as an adult, wrote about, and they particularize the kind of social history that is discussed in Chapter 7. The evidence presented in Chapter 8 shows just how impermanent the society Wilder described in her novels really was. Large segments of the population moved frequently, and De Smet was merely a waystation for many families and individuals as they spread out along the frontier during the late nineteenth century. The Couse Opera House served as a center of community activity for many years, opening in 1886, the year after Laura Ingalls and Almanzo Wilder were married. Although we do not know whether they ever attended meetings or performances held there, we can be sure that they knew about it and reasonably certain that they did participate in some of the activities that went on there. The many social activities discussed in this chapter make abundantly clear just how streamlined a narrative Wilder wrote and how much social history was left out of her novels. Finally, Chapter 10 compares and contrasts two artistic visions of the Dakota prairie—the literary rendition of Laura Ingalls Wilder and the prairie paintings of Harvey Dunn. More joined the two artists than separated them, and both found in the Dakota prairie that surrounded them confirmation for their positive, optimistic attitudes toward life.

In reading and interpreting Wilder's novels, it is necessary to keep in mind that they are the result of a collaborative process between mother and daughter. Yet their basic stuff—the factual material, the characterizations, the places described, the ideas discussed, and the plot lines—are almost entirely the mother's. The specific language, some of the dialogue, and sometimes whole scenes were added by her daughter during the editorial process, but the stories themselves all came out of Laura's experience. These are her books, not Rose's. That, in the end, is what matters.

Portion of a diagram of the business center of De Smet, 1883.
(Redrawn by Steve Mayer from De Smet Leader, September 22,
1883. Copyright © 1987 by the South Dakota State Historical Society. All rights reserved. Reprinted with permission)

2 / Place and Community in Wilder's De Smet

Few authors have done more than Wilder to establish an image of the virtue and superiority of the small-town way of life. Five of her autobiographical novels were set in and around what is now De Smet, South Dakota, even though her initial impressions of the town were anything but approving. As a young teenager unaccustomed to the din and bustle produced by more people than she had ever been around before, Wilder longed to escape the "muddy, cluttered, noisy town" and return to the broad, empty prairie.[1] In a short time, however, a sense of community had become important to her. In the places where people gathered—in stores, saloons, and churches, at Wednesday night prayer meetings, at Ladies Aid sociables and school programs—her characters established and consolidated the bonds of affection and obligation that constitute true community. Every house, every store, every place was associated with its own set of people and activities. People acted and interacted within a context heavily shaped by the buildings, places, and open spaces that made up the town's physical environment.

In an examination of this connection between place and community, De Smet can serve as a microcosm of all the small railroad towns that grew up on the agricultural fron-

This chapter was previously published in *South Dakota History* 16:4 (Winter 1986): 351–72. Copyright © 1987 by the South Dakota State Historical Society. All rights reserved. Reprinted with permission.

tier during the great Dakota boom of the early 1880s. Through Wilder's novels, we can establish the link between place and community, and by supplementing this fictional link with research in newspapers, land records, and other sources, we can develop a more complete picture of the ways in which communal relationships were associated with, resulted from, or were enhanced by particular settings. By looking at the real town of De Smet during the period that Wilder wrote about, we can see that Wilder's portrayal was accurate and that De Smet provides a case study of Robert V. Hine's observation, "Wherever community thrived on the frontier, it was framed by a sense of place."[2]

Wilder herself did not realize the importance of place to her own sense of community and well-being until she left town briefly in the winter of 1883. She had taken her first teaching job at almost sixteen years of age and had to live with a family a dozen miles south of De Smet. Returning home the first weekend to be with her family, she eagerly caught up on news from them and then ran over to visit her friend Mary Power.

> She had quite forgotten that she had ever disliked the town. It was bright and brisk this morning. Sunlight glinted on the icy ruts of snow in the street and sparkled on the frosty edges of the board sidewalk. In the two blocks there were only two vacant lots on the west side of the street now, and some of the stores were painted, white or gray. Harthorne's grocery was painted red. Everywhere there was the stir and bustle of morning. The storekeepers in thick coats and caps were scraping trodden bits of snow from the sidewalk before their stores, and talking and joking as they worked. Doors slammed; hens cackled, and horses whinnied in the stables.[3]

Places that a short time earlier had seemed intimidating and ugly to Wilder now conveyed an entirely different sense. She was older, she was acting out a new role, she saw things in a different perspective. As the storekeepers tipped their caps and greeted her, she felt grown-up. The town's physical presence affected her differently from the way it had earlier; now, the town consisted of more than buildings, streets, and structures. Ultimately, it was the people who inhabited the town that brought it to life, and implicit throughout all of Wilder's writing is this belief in the close connection between place and community.

In 1883, at about the same time that she was beginning to appreciate the town for the first time, a man named O. Swift arrived in De Smet to solicit subscribers for a bird's-eye view of the town. During the late nineteenth century, dozens of artists like Swift worked their way through the Midwest, employed by companies in Chicago and elsewhere that manufactured lithographic views of towns and sold them for anywhere from one dollar to five dollars apiece. Since photographs of early De Smet are almost nonexistent, Swift's drawing provides a useful guide to the physical appearance of the town and can be supplemented with a diagram map published in the De Smet *Leader* in September 1883. This "Diagram of the Business Center of De Smet, Kingsbury County, D.T." locates stores, homes, and other buildings.[4] (Published four and a half months after the bird's-eye view was done, during a time of rapid construction, the diagram includes several new structures that had gone up in the meantime and is not strictly comparable to the earlier depiction.)

The rapid changes in the town's appearance and the flux of its population should be kept firmly in mind when looking at Swift's bird's-eye view. It is tempting to think the picture portrays Laura Ingalls Wilder's De Smet as it "really" was in the same way that some readers think her books represent late-nineteenth-century small-town America as it "really" was. Suffice it to say, no single portrait—visual or verbal—can recapture all that was happening in De Smet or anywhere else. Instead, the bird's-eye view gives us a stylized, standardized view of a typical railroad town of the period. The haste with which this kind of picture was done and the way in which artists

Swift's bird's-eye view of De Smet, 1883.

OF

DAK.

URY COUNTY

Loftus & Broadbent, General Merchandise, Calumet Ave.
Geo. Wilmuth & Co., General Merchandise, Calumet Ave.
Peirson & Cooley, Meat Market, Calumet Ave.
E. R. Bennett, Groceries and Provisions, Calumet Ave.
Peter Holburg, Real Estate Dealer, Calumet Ave.
C. H. Tinkham, Furniture, Calumet Ave.
Lyngby Bros., Blacksmiths, Calumet Ave.
Frank H. Schaub, Harness, etc., Calumet Ave.
H. Hinz, Billiard Parlor, Calumet Ave.
C. S. G. Fuller & Bro., Hardware and Farm Machinery, Calumet Ave.
Horn & McDonald, Editors The News, Calumet Ave.
DeSmet Publishing Co., Publishers The Leader, Calumet Ave.
G. H. Scofield, General Merchandise, Calumet Ave.
J. J. Shockley, Blacksmith, Cor. First St. and Joliet Ave.

(Courtesy South Dakota State Historical Society)

transformed notes and sketches done on ground level into a single drawing imagined from a vantage point high overhead precluded detailed accuracy.

Much got left out of Swift's picture of De Smet. Streets and backyards, for example, were so full of garbage that newspaper editor Mark Brown was constantly chiding his readers for failing to clean up their places. Indeed, several days before the artist arrived on the scene, a dead calf could be seen lying on the ground west of the Kingsbury House barn.[5] "It seems to be necessary to keep on howling for a general cleaning up," Brown scolded a week later. "There are some scandalous back yards in this village. Do have some style about you, friends."[6] Nevertheless, we see no garbage in Swift's rendition, nor any sidewalks, paths, shrubs, bushes, flowers, gardens, weeds, fences, dogs, cows, farm implements, or wagons—although they were all there. Nor do we see any people. Conversely, if the artist was guilty of leaving some things out of the picture, he can likewise be accused of adding things that were not there. The perfect symmetry of the trees was a product of the artist's imagination, as were the neat stacks of lumber at the yards, which, according to newspaper reports, were constantly bare of that hotly desired commodity all through a year of intense building. The demand was so great that by the end of 1883, a third lumber yard was in operation.[7]

De Smet, like approximately 80 percent of the towns established in eastern Dakota Territory during the 1880s, was a railroad town, and like the others, its appearance and character were heavily influenced by that fact. During 1879 and 1880, as the Chicago and North Western Railroad extended its Dakota Central branch from Tracy, Minnesota, to Pierre on the Missouri River, it established a number of small towns along the route, including De Smet, which was named for Pierre-Jean de Smet, a Jesuit priest from Belgium who served as a missionary to Indians on the plains and in the northwest during the 1840s to 1860s. For all of these towns, the railroad utilized a simple and efficient town design.[8] The townscapes that emerged therefore resulted in part from this deliberate planning, but certainly the countless decisions made by hundreds of individuals seeking their own interest also had an effect.[9] Although no single person or group dictated a town's entire development, similar needs and outlooks did generate similar outcomes, even if the process followed to achieve those results was not a conscious one. "No group sets out to create a landscape," John Brinckerhoff Jackson reminds us. "What it sets out to do is to create a community, and the landscape as its visible manifestation is simply the by-product of people working and living, sometimes coming together, sometimes staying apart, but always recognizing their interdependence."[10] Thus, a reciprocal process was operating: out of the search for community, the townscape emerged; within the places making up that townscape, community was established and reinforced.

De Smet is laid out in the shape of the letter T. The main street forms its base, with the railroad as its crossbar.[11] Like every other town on the Dakota Central line between Elkton and Pierre, De Smet's main street ran perpendicular to the tracks. The basic formula used by the railroad for laying out towns west to Huron varied only in size and detail, with towns that were expected to grow receiving bigger initial layouts. West of Huron, other surveyors adhered to the same general pattern, making it impossible to distinguish towns laid out by the railroad from those platted by private parties.[12]

With few exceptions, surveyors used standard lot and street dimensions that had been established in towns farther east. Arthur Jacobi, a surveyor employed by the railroad, staked out the town in lots and blocks by March 27, 1880, as recorded in the official county records. The original plat of De Smet included just four blocks, each 350 feet square. Calumet Avenue, or Main Street, was 100 feet wide and ran perpendicular to the railroad tracks. First Street, running alongside the right-of-way and depot facilities, was also 100 feet in width. With the exception of Joliet Avenue, the other streets were 80 feet wide. The busi-

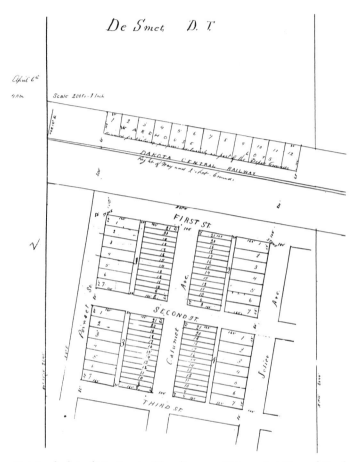

Original plat of De Smet, 1880. (Source: "Town Lot Record Book
No. 1, Kingsbury County, 1879–1887," pp. 3–4, Kingsbury
County Courthouse, De Smet, South Dakota)

ness lots along Calumet Avenue, fourteen on each side of
the street per block, were a standard 25 feet in width.
Their 165-foot depth, usual in towns along the Dakota
Central, made them longer than their counterparts in
many places. Residential lots on side streets, seven to the
block, were 50 feet wide. Twenty-foot alleys bisected each
block. The north-south streets were named Poinset (or

Poinsett), Calumet, and Joliet; the east-west streets were numbered—First, Second, and Third. Across the tracks to the north, warehouse lots were set aside for railroad use.[13]

Town planners can foster a sense of community by providing public parks and other spaces in which people can meet and interact, but the Chicago and North Western apparently attached little importance to such amenities. In De Smet, the railroad adhered to its general practice and made no provisions for setting aside lots for such purposes.[14] Not until after the turn of the century would a park be laid out on railroad land near the depot and an effort made to build other park facilities in town. Meanwhile, baseball diamonds, picnic spots, horse-racing tracks, and other places for games and recreation were located on empty lots in town and in privately owned groves of trees in the country.

The most important public building in a county-seat town like De Smet, of course, is the courthouse. Throughout the South and much of the Midwest, courthouses sitting on central squares or other prominent locations attracted people, who gathered to talk, do business, or just sit for a spell.[15] Courthouse squares, often the geographic centers of towns, also served as communal centers. But where does one put the courthouse in a T-town like De Smet? There is no obvious central location, unless one decides to put it at the opposite end of town from the railroad tracks, with the main street leading up to it. In De Smet (as in all other county-seat towns east of the Missouri River on the line of the Dakota Central), the courthouse was shunted off to the side of Main Street. Swift's bird's-eye view shows the courthouse square one block east of Calumet Avenue near the railroad tracks. In 1883, the small jail building that occupied the spot was all the town could afford. Newspaper editor Mark Brown found the situation deplorable and observed: "At present all the record books stand on shelves in the register's office, where a fire would leave no vestige of them. Every land title in the county is in peril every day."[16] A rather picturesque courthouse was finally built in 1898, but other buildings were used to house the functions of county government in the meantime. The first session of county court, held in 1883, took place in the new flour mill south of the railroad tracks, which stood empty while the owner waited for his machinery to arrive.[17] Even after the courthouse was built, its peripheral location reduced its drawing power as a gathering spot and reinforced the townspeople's normal tendency to gravitate to the stores on the main street. Flowers and trees were planted and curved walkways added to the grounds, but the courthouse square never became the attraction for bench sitters and conversationalists that courthouses in other areas of the country did.

T-towns developed along two axes—the railroad and Main Street. The facilities along the railroad tracks in De Smet resembled those in other railroad towns. Water-guzzling steam engines filled their boilers from a tank standing west of the depot. As in other towns where housing was scarce during the early days, De Smet had a two-story depot, which allowed the agent to live with his family on the second floor.[18] The depot was one of the town's "hot spots"—a gathering place where people often stopped just to chat and watch the trains come and go. Here one could see enacted the little rituals of community that reinforced the ties which bound people to each other. In *Little Town on the Prairie*, Wilder describes one such event, a party at the depot given by her classmate, Benjamin Woodworth. After eating oranges and oyster soup with their meal in the upstairs living quarters, the teenagers trooped downstairs to play games in the waiting room until the clock struck ten.[19]

Another center for gossip was the Seefield grain elevator next door, where farmers discussed prices and the weather when they brought their grain to market. The two lumber yards located on the north side of the tracks remained extremely busy all through 1883. Farther down the tracks was G. W. Elliott's new mill, which was under construction when the bird's-eye artist arrived in town. The decision to build it illustrated the informal, democratic decision-making process that often operated in frontier communities. After arriving in town in March, Elliott, an inventive go-getter from Owatonna, Minnesota, offered to build a custom mill if the townspeople would donate the land along with a $1,000 bonus to help him get started. A group consisting of most of the town's businessmen met at Couse's hardware store to consider the proposition, and after agreeing to go ahead, they managed to raise half the necessary money in two weeks' time.[20]

No place better represented the spirit of excitement and change in frontier towns like De Smet than did the hotels, which were also located near the tracks for the convenience of travelers. In 1883, De Smet could boast two hotels—the Kingsbury House and the Exchange Hotel—both situated in the block south of the railroad tracks on the west side of Calumet Avenue. Patrons boarded family style, and with the crush of homesteaders flooding into town that spring, they made sure to come early at mealtimes unless they wanted to wait for the first comers to finish. Cigar smoke filled the air. Loud exclamations and guffaws punctuated the jokes and boisterous arguments of the mostly male clientele. The Exchange Hotel was probably the most active social center in town that year,[21] and checkers was a favorite pastime for the lodgers and townspeople there. Across the street, editor Mark Brown often got an earful of the wild goings-on in the hotels. "The blood-curdling debauchery known as checkers is indulged in to an alarming extent just over the way," he observed in one of his local paragraphs, "and the mad hilarity it evokes at times would frighten a wooden Indian into hysterics."[22]

The railroad and the facilities associated with it constituted the town's major link to the outside world and directed people's attention outward, while Main Street directed their attention to the local scene. More than in the churches, more than in the schools, more than anywhere else, Main Street was the place where everybody congregated—transacting business, discussing the weather, or just passing the time of day. It was here that people en-

Looking north on De Smet's Main Street (Calumet Avenue) around the turn of the century. *(Courtesy South Dakota State Historical Society)*

gaged most actively in face-to-face contacts and here that community found its fullest realization.

Just three years old in 1883, De Smet's Main Street displayed the characteristics of a frontier town, but one that was gradually acquiring the accoutrements and comforts of civilization. Buildings that had been hurriedly fashioned out of lumber a year or two earlier had been painted, and in many cases, additions or second stories were being constructed. Most of the stores had false fronts, which came in two basic styles, one rectangular in shape (and flat on top), the other pointed in the middle. Whether false fronts were used because it was easier to saw boards square than to fit them to a sloping roof, because they pro-

vided more space for painting signs, or because they ful-
filled the owners' pretensions is impossible to discern.
Probably De Smetites gave the matter little thought, since
false fronts were the style of the period, a part of the cultural baggage residents had brought with them. The false-
front store was a communal aesthetic, something agreed
upon without explicit consideration.[23] It said: "This is
who I am and this is who we are. We are this way because
this is the way things are supposed to be done." Since everything else was simple and functional in the early days,
false fronts, unadorned as they were, provided just about
the only architectural flourish to be found in De Smet in
1883. Store buildings had no fancy windows fixed up with
alluring displays. Businesses were essentially boxes punctuated with windows to let in sunlight and fresh air.

Despite its architectural shortcomings, Main Street was
the place where community identity was forged. It was the
part of town visitors noticed when passing through on the
railroad and the place where most village activity occurred. Towns the size of De Smet usually had two blocks
of stores on Main Street, with some spillover to adjoining
streets. Smaller towns were capable of supporting only
one block of stores, and large ones such as Huron had
three or more. On Main Street many types of businesses
existed side by side in no special arrangement, with two
major exceptions. Hotels usually sprang up near the
tracks, and banks generally were built on corner lots,
which were considered the most desirable since they received the most traffic. Banks often bid premium prices
for them at opening-day auctions when the first lots were
sold, and in 1883, both of De Smet's banks were located on
corners: the Kingsbury County Bank, on the northwest
corner of Calumet Avenue and Third Street, and the Bank
of De Smet on the northeast corner of Calumet Avenue
and Second Street, across the street from Pa Ingalls' store.

During the early years, most of the Main Street stores
were one story or one and one-half stories high. In *Little
Town on the Prairie*, Wilder mentioned several genuine
two-story buildings, including Mead's and Beardsley's ho-

Charles Tinkham in his furniture store in the 1920s. *(Courtesy South Dakota State Historical Society)*

tels (in 1883, the Exchange and Kingsbury hotels, respectively) and Tinkham's furniture store. Charles H. Tinkham was a twenty-six-year-old cabinetmaker from the state of Maine when he walked from what was then the end of the line at Volga to the fledgling village of De Smet thirty-five miles to the west. He remained a fixture in the community for over half a century, outliving most of his fellow storekeepers. Like many other furniture dealers, he was also a mortician or funeral director, and it was in the Tinkhams' second-floor living quarters above the store that Laura and her friend Mary Power attended a rather boring dime sociable sponsored by the Ladies Aid Society in 1881.[24]

Wilder's novels provide a fairly detailed and accurate, though naturally selective, description of "the little town on the prairie." When Wilder mentioned the businesses and other buildings in town, it was usually as the scene of some kind of activity or social doing rather than a simple description. One memorable incident occurred during a blizzard, when she and her classmates got lost and almost wandered out onto the prairie beyond the edge of town. Recognizing Mead's hotel at the north end of Main Street, the group was able to get home by walking from one building to the next in the storm—Hinz's saloon, Royal Wilder's feed store, Barker's grocery, the Beardsley hotel, Couse's hardware, Fuller's hardware, Bradley's drugstore, and Power's tailor shop were all welcome sights.[25] In this episode, the buildings on Main Street literally saved the lives of Laura and her schoolmates; as a general rule, these buildings were the places where life was lived, business transacted, and societal rituals enacted.

Day after day, Wilder observed people talking in front of stores, teams patiently waiting at hitching posts, and storekeepers filling grocery orders for their customers. In this commonplace round of daily living could be found the core of community life in De Smet. During the hard winter of 1880-1881, men gathered daily at Fuller's hardware store to learn the latest news and to while away the dreary hours. Favorite pastimes of the many bachelors in town for the winter were checkers and cards, often played at the hotels or at Bradley's drugstore. The saloons, when they were open, provided another way to relieve boredom, but scuffles and shouting sometimes broke the quiet.[26] Every place in town—saloon, depot, store, church, school, home—had human associations and meanings for Laura and her neighbors, and within these confines a sense of community was established.

Reflecting this community spirit and boosting the town's prospects were its two newspapers, the De Smet *News*, established at the time the town was founded in 1880, and the De Smet *Leader*, initiated three years later. The offices of both newspapers were located on the east side of Main Street, and contrary to what often happened elsewhere, the editors got along amicably and did not train their editorial guns at each other. Both naturally boosted the town and predicted great things for it, but their most important function was informing their readers about local happenings. The brief paragraphs that made up the local news often contained personal and rather intimate information about townspeople. From them, readers might learn whose house was being painted, what caused Wednesday night's fight at the saloon, and why people were complaining about their taxes. Newspapers extended the reach of the gossip that constantly went on in stores, on the sidewalks, and in people's homes.

In the age of the horse, hitching posts symbolized the mode of transportation that kept people close to home most of the time and kept things moving at a relatively slow pace, and every town also had its livery stables, blacksmiths, and draymen. At the south end of Calumet Avenue, the Fonger brothers ran a livery stable until they sold out toward the end of 1883 to White and Pierson. This place must have made an impression on Laura, because she mentioned it several times in her novels (spelling it Pearson's) and included it on a map she drew of the town to help her while writing. She remembered it as the last building they had to pass on Main Street before they turned off to the southeast to head out to their homestead. Christian Lyngbye operated a blacksmith shop across the street from Pierson's,[27] and two other blacksmiths had shops on Joliet Avenue near the railroad tracks. As in other towns, these liveries and blacksmiths were located on the periphery of the main business section.

A couple blocks west of Main Street were the elementary school and the Congregational church. Besides providing the setting for instruction, the school symbolized people's commitment to democracy and their faith in the future. There, Wilder and her classmates not only learned basic skills but also absorbed traditional values and were socialized into the community. Wilder also retained vivid memories of the "literaries" held in the schoolhouse on cold winter evenings. Everybody in town, it seemed, would turn out to listen to debates on the temperance question or women's suffrage or some less serious issue.[28]

The church was another spot for social gatherings as well as for church services for the Congregationalists and for the Methodists and the Baptists until they were able to build their own edifices. The Catholics held services in the schoolhouse once a month until they were able to build a church. Several literaries were also held in the church in 1883.[29] With ministers in scarce supply on the frontier, people had to be satisfied with services every two or three weeks, and necessity paved the way for interdenominational cooperation. Revivals drew townspeople and farm families from miles around. Wilder vividly recreated one meeting when the preaching of Rev. Edward Brown sent shivers up her spine and over her scalp. Although neither she nor her parents much liked Reverend Brown, he seemed to have been well regarded in the community.[30]

The installation of a 400-pound bell in the church belfry in December 1883 symbolized the arrival of civilization in the fledgling town. "This is the first church bell in Kingsbury County," noted Mark Brown, the preacher's son. "So, one after another the institutions, the refinements, the social, intellectual and religious privileges of America's Christian civilization become naturalized and at home where only four years since was but a vast wilderness of prairie grass, whitened by the bones of the bison, and the poles of Indian wigwams still standing, but now filled with a population of intelligent, moral and enterprising people."[31]

In the early years, while the town was without a public meeting place, the school and church were also frequently pressed into service to accommodate a surprising number of traveling road shows, speeches, suppers, dances, and other events. After 1886, when Edward H. Couse, the hardware man, built his new brick store with an opera house on the second floor, it became the center for dances, high-school graduations, Memorial Day services, revival meetings, and entertainments (see Chapter 9). There, the community gathered on many occasions and in many guises to reinforce its bonds of fellowship and to reenact the rituals of solidarity.

Of course, any attempt to understand the degree to

which community existed in small midwestern railroad towns a century ago is fraught with difficulties, and no definitive conclusions are possible. But because of the detailed memories Laura Ingalls Wilder preserved in her novels, we can learn more about the place and community of De Smet than about other small towns of the era. And to the extent that true community did exist in De Smet, we can be certain that it was heavily influenced by the physical setting that Wilder describes. In the stores, the streets, the homes, churches, and schools, at the depot and the grain elevators, under the trees and at the baseball diamonds, on the sidewalks and everywhere that people went, their interactions formed the relationships that determined what kind of community existed in De Smet. In the 1880s, Wilder and her neighbors developed a sense of place that affected their thoughts and activities. That awareness of place and the community interaction associated with it lingered in Wilder's memory decades later and helped her to shape her recollections of small-town life.

3 / Freedom and Control in Fact and Fiction

In addition to faith in the future, the virtues of persistence and hard work, the beneficence and occasional destructiveness of nature, the centrality of family, the search for community, the importance of freedom is a dominant theme of Laura Ingalls Wilder's books for children.[1] But Wilder never conceives of this freedom as an absolute; rather, it is subject to a variety of constraints—external and internal—that interact with it in uneasy tension. The Ingalls family moved west to Dakota Territory in 1879 because of Pa's quest for freedom from the constrictions hemming him in on the more settled frontier. Farther west, he believed, people could exercise greater control over their lives and in so doing fulfill their destinies. People could make a decent living on a homestead in the West. "The hunting's good in the west, a man can get all the meat he wants," Charles cheerfully told his wife Caroline.[2]

After four years in Dakota Territory, Pa's westering urge had not diminished. "I would like to go West," he told Ma one day. "A fellow doesn't have room to breathe here any more." But she was having none of it. She had been willing to come to De Smet, a town on the Chicago and North Western Railroad in eastern Dakota Territory, but intended to go no farther. "Oh, Charles!" she exclaimed. "I was so tired of being dragged from pillar to post, and I

This chapter was previously published in *Great Plains Quarterly* 9 (Winter 1989): 27–35. Reprinted with permission.

The Ingalls family in 1894. *Sitting:* Ma (Caroline), Pa (Charles), and Mary. *Standing:* Carrie, Laura, and Grace. *(Courtesy South Dakota State Historical Society)*

thought we were settled here.''[3] The parents' disagreement over the desirability of the settled life versus a continual push toward the edge of the frontier is one of the central tensions providing interest and continuity in the Little House series. Pa yearned for the freedom to be found over the horizon; Ma sought it in settled surroundings. Pa in many ways represented the typical frontiersman—willful, self-sufficient, industrious, and above all individualistic. Ma on the other hand reflected submissiveness, self-abnegation, and commitment to the larger whole. Yet, such dichotomies can never be neat or complete. Both husband and wife desired freedom in their own ways, and both recognized the need for and sought to establish the kind of control over their lives and their surroundings that would enable them to realize their dreams.[4]

Laura's personality closely resembled that of her father; her older sister Mary's resembled their mother's. Laura thrilled at the prospect of moving West. Thinking of the Wessington Hills to the west and the mysterious shadow they presented against the sky, she ''wanted to travel on and on, over those miles, and see what lay beyond the hills." Laura's discomfort at being thrown among so many people when the family first moved to De Smet reminded her of a passage from the Bible about the wings of a bird and, as Wilder wrote, "if she had the wings of a bird, she, too, would have spread them and flown, fast, fast, far away." Laura's desire to be independent and free as a bird manifested itself in many ways. She loved horses and though she was frightened a little at first, she enjoyed driving the young frisky colts out over the prairie. Almanzo Wilder won her affections, in large measure, because of the sleigh and buggy rides he offered her. Sometimes it must have seemed that she was more interested in the horses than in Almanzo. When storms blew up on the treeless, unprotected prairie, Laura appreciated the safety of the cellar, but "she could hardly bear the closed-in, underground feeling of it." Thus, when she insisted on leaving out of her wedding ceremony the traditional promise to love and obey Almanzo, she was playing out the role stamped indelibly by her character.[5]

Laura admired her sister Mary but could not be like her. When Mary went blind after a severe illness, it only seemed to accentuate the older girl's patience, self-control, and underlying goodness.

> "I wish I could be like you. But I guess I never can be," Laura sighed. "I don't know how you can be so good."
>
> "I'm not really," Mary told her. "I do try, but if you could see how rebellious and mean I feel sometimes, if you could see what I really am, inside, you wouldn't want to be like me."
>
> "I *can* see what you're like inside," Laura contradicted. "It shows all the time. You're always perfectly patient and never the least bit mean."[6]

Mary, because she was blind, understood that appearances deceive. Her own character was more complex than any broad brush strokes could adequately portray, and likewise the everyday lives that people lived in De Smet carried within them their own contradictions. Laura's and Pa's quests for freedom cannot be considered the polar opposite of submission to control. Rather, we must recognize that on the frontier, freedom and control were interpenetrating—albeit contradictory—forces that simultaneously pushed people in different directions. After all, when Ma complained to Pa, "I thought we were settled here," his response was: "Well, I guess we are, Caroline. Don't fret. It's just that my wandering foot gets to itching, I guess.'"[7] He reconciled himself to staying put in De Smet, although the urge to move never completely left him.

Laura understood just how her father felt, for she too accepted the need to sacrifice her own personal inclinations for the good of the family. Nothing appealed less to her than teaching school, but because she realized it was the best and practically only way she could earn money to help send Mary to college, she reluctantly did it. Laura responded to duty just as her father did: "He must stay in a settled country for the sake of them all, just as she must teach school again, though she did so hate to be shut into a school room.'"[8]

Writing her autobiographical novels fifty years later, Wilder clearly understood that living in the frontier environment entailed a web of duties and obligations, requirements that for most settlers heavily outweighed the kinds of freedom or independence it facilitated. Efforts to establish control over the environment, economic conditions, social interactions, and personal inclinations were central ingredients in everyone's lives. All of these impulses interconnected, so if we endeavor to understand the many ways individuals attempted to establish control over their lives, we may better understand the frontier agricultural society that is the setting for Wilder's novels.

Any such enterprise inevitably starts with Frederick Jackson Turner and his frontier thesis, enunciated at the American Historical Association convention in Chicago in 1893, a year before Wilder and her husband finally left

De Smet to go to Missouri. America's historical development and the features that distinguished it from Europe, Turner asserted, could be explained by the "existence of an area of free land, its continuous recession, and the advance of American settlement westward."[9]

The most obvious characteristic of the frontiersman, in Turner's scheme, was individualism. Here was a supremely self-reliant character, independent in thought and action, with boundless confidence in the future. Self-reliance and optimism were the positive features of individualism, but they also bred impatience at restraint, suspicion of government, and restlessness under authority. Civilization stifled people, according to Turner's frontiersman, who therefore opposed all order and restraint and saw little need for education and tradition. Instead, he retreated to the family unit, which resulted in an atomistic society.[10]

Turner was not the first to stress American individualism. During the 1830s Alexis de Tocqueville, individualism's classic explicator, helped introduce the concept. "Individualism," he wrote, "is a calm and considered feeling which disposes each citizen to isolate himself from the mass of his fellows and withdraw into the circle of family and friends; with this little society formed to his taste, he gladly leaves the greater society to look after itself." He also observed that "each man is forever thrown back on himself alone, and there is danger that he may be shut up in the solitude of his own heart." Drawing on the Tocquevillean tradition, a noteworthy analyst of American society expressed the concern "that this individualism may have grown cancerous—that it may be destroying those social integuments that Tocqueville saw as moderating its more destructive potentialities, that it may be threatening the survival of freedom itself."[11]

Even though individualism did characterize Americans on the frontier, countervailing forces of control were as pervasive, insistent, and ultimately influential on people's behavior. Charles Beard once noted that on the frontier many individuals could be found, but little individualism, and Wilder's novels illustrate how individualism could be a less important factor in people's behavior in a town like De Smet than their efforts to establish control. Historians have noted that the force of traditional controls and values declines in a frontier social environment,[12] which makes it all the more imperative for people to reassert social control. But the term "social control" does not fully encompass the processes that were operating in the West.

On the frontier the first priority was to establish control over the environment and forces of nature in order to ensure basic physical survival. Settlers had to obtain food, construct shelter, and protect themselves from wild animals and the elements. Pa Ingalls' assertion that a man with a gun in the West could get all the meat he wanted proved overly optimistic. The arrival of the settlers pushed bison and antelope farther west, and a hunter could not support a family on occasional jackrabbits and game birds. He had to wrest a living from the land. A family had to plant a garden and buy staples at the store, and if a family didn't have enough money, it might suffer from malnutrition.

During the long winter of 1880-1881, when all trains from the east were blocked for months, the Ingalls family got tired of living on potatoes and brown bread, but they were lucky to have them.[13] When the newly built town on the prairie nearly ran out of wheat, Almanzo Wilder and his friend Cap Garland risked their lives to ride twenty miles over snowswept prairies devoid of landmarks to find a settler who, according to rumor, had some wheat he might sell. When they got to his shanty, his initial response to their request to buy wheat to feed starving women and children epitomized the self-sufficient individualism that has been attributed to frontiersmen. "That's not my lookout," he said. "Nobody's responsible for other folks that haven't got enough forethought to take care of themselves."

Having persuaded the man to part with sixty bushels by offering him $1.25 a bushel for them, the two barely man-

De Smetites stop for a picture at the north end of Main Street during a celebration in the 1880s. *(Courtesy South Dakota State Historical Society)*

aged to make it back to town. Daniel Loftus, the storekeeper who had sent them on their errand, immediately tried to bilk the townspeople by upping the price to $3.00 a bushel. When a delegation led by Charles Ingalls complained, Loftus said, "The wheat's mine and I've got a right to charge any price I want for it."

"That's so Loftus, you have," Ingalls replied. "This is a free country and every man's got a right to do as he pleases with his own property." But in this case, he continued, circumstances were different. The well-being of the community was involved, and whatever Loftus did now would long be remembered by everyone gathered there. Gerald Fuller, the hardware man, chimed in, "You got to treat folks right or you won't last long in business, not in this country." The will—or tyranny—of the majority carried the day, and Loftus was a beaten man. He agreed to sell the wheat for the $1.25 he had paid for it.[14] Whether the story is historically accurate or not, Loftus did become the most prominent storekeeper in town during the next forty years, active in civic affairs, prominent in the state retailers' association, and successful in business.[15] The episode illustrates several aspects of control: the dangers imposed by climate and environment, the usefulness of physical strength and bravery in overcoming those elements, the lack of roads and landmarks imposing control on the landscape, the importance of money, the centrality of gossip as a means of establishing consensus in the community, and the force of public opinion.

After a few years, garden vegetables, chickens, pigs, grain, and other foods helped the Ingallses forget the rapid depletion of game,[16] but there was always the danger of crop failure, which recurred frequently. During these lean years, tables were set more sparsely, even though starvation was no longer a danger. Shelter, too, had to be provided. The titles of Wilder's novels, as well as their contents, reflect the importance of buildings. In the little houses that were home to her she found warmth and comfort, both physical and emotional. Whether it was a dugout in a hillside, a tarpaper claim shanty, a store building in town, or a snug house with manufactured windows, the walls surrounding Laura provided protection from cold and rain and wolves. Nature was two-faced to her: on the one side beautiful and inspirational, on the other full of danger. It seemed to Laura sometimes that the storms were alive, sounding like packs of wolves or panthers, trying to attack. Ma advised that since they couldn't do anything about the storms, they should take them as they came, but Pa shouted his defiance at them when he was cooped up more than he could stand. "Howl! blast you! howl!" he called back. "We're all here safe! You can't get at us!"[17]

The threat of wild animals was more imaginary than real, but caution was advisable. Coyotes posed no serious danger to people or farm animals, and wolves generally retreated as the settlers advanced, but once after she and Almanzo were married, Laura grabbed a pitchfork to chase away wolves that threatened their sheep. Gophers sometimes got into the corn and blackbirds into the oats. Ma and the girls vainly tried to scare the blackbirds away with shouts and brooms, but even in defeat, Ma found some consolation, baking some delicious blackbird pies for dinner. Her comment, "There's no great loss without some small gain," typified her approach to life. If she couldn't control a situation, she would redefine it, looking for the cheerful aspects of otherwise dreary circumstances.[18]

Farmers and townspeople waged a constant battle to keep their farms and businesses, and the outcome was always in doubt. Still, all of Wilder's novels remain steadfastly optimistic about the future, with the partial exception of *The First Four Years*. Dakota Territory was "next year country," and people who lacked faith in the future did not stay around long. But the difficulties of wresting a living from the land were always pressing. And if the farmers did not make it, the storekeepers in town could not make it either.

Agriculture during the 1880s was moving through a transitional phase as mechanization rapidly replaced human labor. "Agricultural machinery is going off like hotcakes, and the smile of the dealer is broad and bland," the De Smet *Leader* reported in March 1883.[19] Mechanization proved beneficial in that it conferred on the farmers greater physical control over their situation. With its advantages came further complications, however, that actually left them with less control over their total situation. Machinery was rarely ever paid for in cash, and the debts and mortgages that accompanied the new reapers, binders, and cultivators saddled the farmers with a burden that was hard to escape. Many of them mortgaged their land, whether it had been purchased or homesteaded originally, because crop prices often lagged behind the expenses involved in planting and harvesting.

After disastrous experiences with buying on credit at Plum Creek, Laura's father was careful to stay out of debt, recognizing how easy it was to get sucked deeper and deeper into the morass.[20] His son-in-law Almanzo, however, saw no way to avoid debt and remained continually hopeful that the next crop would turn his and Laura's financial affairs around. The arithmetic of farming was often discouraging. When interest on chattel mortgages was 3 percent per month, the calculations led almost certainly to disaster. No wonder Laura, who had started out liking her family's claim and hating the town, ended up liking the town and hating farm life after marriage: "She hated the farm and the stock and the smelly lambs, the cooking of food and the dirty dishes. Oh, she hated it all, and especially the debts that must be paid whether she could work or not."[21] The tone of *The First Four Years* differs considerably from that of the earlier books. The sense of optimism, while present, is muted. Laura as a married women no longer could depend upon her parents to take care of things, and concerns about the future came to the fore. She kept the manuscript of *The First Four Years* hidden away, and it was published only when it was discovered after her death.[22]

Along with new farm machinery, other technological innovations made work easier for people and allowed them greater control over their lives. But here, too, there were trade-offs. Kerosene lit the lamps of the Ingalls family during the hard winter, but when the trains stopped running because of bad weather, the kerosene ran out and they discovered they had become dependent upon it. "If only I had some grease I could fix some kind of a light," Ma said. "We didn't lack for light when I was a girl, before this newfangled kerosene was ever heard of." Pa agreed: "These times are too progressive. Everything has changed too fast. Railroads and telegraph and kerosene and coal stoves—they're good things to have but the trouble is, folks get to depend on 'em."[23]

Even with new labor-saving devices, people relied heavily on human muscle power to get their work done. During the hard winter, gangs of snow shovelers walked down the line trying to clear the railroad tracks so the trains could get through. The family twisted hay into sticks to burn in the stove and laboriously ground wheat in a coffee grinder until their muscles ached. Farm work remained backbreaking labor, something Laura learned from experience helping first her father and later her husband in the fields.[24]

From a very early age, Laura played an important economic role in the family and quickly felt an obligation to contribute to the family's economic well-being. Whatever money she could earn would increase the family's ability to control its destiny. Thus, she accepted the need to take in boarders as settlers streamed into the region, even though she was afraid of the rough men who stayed under their roof. The family temporarily lost some control over its daily life but came out $42.50 ahead in the process, money that could be used for sending Mary to college so she could become a schoolteacher. It was this goal that spurred Laura on—that drove her to work as a seamstress for twenty-five cents a day, to stay with a woman on her claim north of Manchester, and to take several teaching jobs despite her wish not to do so. "If she studied hard and faithfully," she thought, "and got a teacher's certificate, and then got a school to teach, she would be a real help to Pa and Ma. Then she could begin to repay them for all that it had cost to provide for her since she was a baby. Then, surely, they could send Mary to college."[25]

On the frontier, hard work was both a family duty and a personal obligation. The work ethic was ingrained in people through the socialization process,[26] but if that or family obligations were not enough of a spur, economic necessity usually did the trick. Pa liked to say that he had made a fourteen-dollar bet—the cost of the filing fee—with Uncle Sam that he could hold out on his 160-acre homestead for five years before he gave up.[27] Many settlers lost their bet. Pa won his but never achieved prosperity, spending many of his later years doing carpentry and other jobs around De Smet.[28] Laura and Almanzo got married just as the wet years gave way to the dry and just as the floor began to drop out of farm prices. By the time they finally gave up (just after the period covered in *The First Four Years*), the Farmers' Alliance was active in Dakota Territory and the Populist party was about to be born.

By 1889 the homestead had been sold off, hot winds had killed the wheat and the oats, their second child had died shortly after birth, a tornado had struck, and a fire had burned down their farmhouse. Their only hope for getting out of debt and holding on to their land was getting a good crop the next year—something they had prayed for during the first four years but never obtained. Considering all of the problems, Laura realized that

> it would be a fight to win out in this business of farming, but strangely she felt her spirit rising for the struggle. The incurable optimism of the farmer who throws his seed on the ground every spring, betting it and his time against the elements, seemed inextricably to blend with the creed of her pioneer forefathers that "it is better farther on"—only instead of farther on in space, it was farther on in time, over the horizon of the years ahead instead of the far horizon of the west.[29]

By then Laura had given up her childhood dreams of going farther west to find freedom and happiness, and had invested her hopes in realizing her dreams over the horizon of tomorrow. Ironically, she and Almanzo *did* decide to make a geographic move—to the southeast, to Mansfield, Missouri, where they would live the rest of their lives.

Unable to control their economic destiny as farmers, Laura and Almanzo sought some measure of control over themselves and their situation. That effort to achieve control is a theme that Wilder wove through her later books. Her account of her first teaching job at the Brewster school, south of De Smet, illustrates several aspects of this process. Only fifteen years old at the time, she approached the job with trepidation. She worried that the children wouldn't mind her—that she wouldn't be able to control them—but her father reassured her by reminding her that she had never failed at anything she had tried. He also reiterated the need for self-control. "You are so quick, flutterbudget," he told her. "You are apt to act or speak first, and think afterward. Now you must do your thinking first and speak afterward. If you will remember to do that, you will not have any trouble."[30]

Controlling one's emotions was a lesson taught early in the Ingalls family. That a "grown-up person must never let feelings be shown by voice or manner" was a principle the girls all learned. By the time they were grown, they usually followed it. "Modulate your voice, Laura," Ma would remind her. When Laura's spiteful statement about Nellie Oleson's country parents led to an incident between the two girls, Ma wrote some advice in Laura's album that she could keep forever:

> If wisdom's ways you wisely seek,
> Five things observe with care.
> To whom you speak,
> Of whom you speak,
> And how, and when, and where.[31]

Memory work provided another source of self-discipline for Laura. Along with the Psalms, Laura memorized the Declaration of Independence and the exports of Brazil. At the singing school held in the Congregational church, Mr. Clewett drilled his pupils up and down the scales to improve their voices. Living each day was an exercise in exerting discipline over one's emotions and inclinations. Once Laura slacked off in her studies and obtained only a 99 in history and a 92 in English; that experience convinced her that there could be no more self-indulgence. And when she thought she could not bear to return to stay with the Brewsters, who were constantly fighting with each other, she simply told herself that everything must go on.[32]

Although Laura's child's-eye view of De Smet falls short of a full sociological portrait of the town, it does identify the problem that probably did most to challenge community norms, the liquor issue. In towns like De Smet, the temperance forces would manage to shut down the saloons one day; then the next day the liquor interests would reverse the decision at the polls. At bottom, the liquor issue was one of control—by one group of people over another and by individuals over their own actions. Pa Ingalls sided with the prohibition camp. "Two saloons in this town are just two saloons too many," he said.[33]

Nowhere else do a society's instruments of control ex-

pose themselves so dramatically as in its rituals and celebrations, and with the possible exception of Christmas,
the Fourth of July was the most anticipated celebration of
the year in American frontier towns. People loaded themselves into wagons and buggies and drove miles into town
to join the ceremonies, fun, and games on Independence
Day.[34] In her draft of the chapter on the Fourth of July celebration held during the second year of the town's existence, Wilder mentioned the reading of the Declaration of
Independence and the typical flowery oration that
"twisted the lion's tail" and "made the eagle scream."[35]
Lane greatly extended the dramatic potential of the episode Wilder described and used it to teach a lesson about
the relationship between freedom and responsibility.

After the songs and the speeches were over, according to
the final, printed version of the book, Laura pondered the
notion that God is America's king.

> Americans won't obey any king on earth. Americans
> are free. That means they have to obey their own con-
> sciences. No king bosses Pa; he has to boss himself.
> Why (she thought), when I am a little older, Pa and
> Ma will stop telling me what to do, and there isn't
> anyone who has a right to give me orders. I will have
> to make myself be good.

Thus were opposites joined: Freedom did not constitute
license; it implied self-discipline.

> Her whole mind seemed to be lighted up by that
> thought. This is what it means to be free. It means,
> you have to be good. "Our father's God, author of lib-
> erty—" The laws of Nature and of Nature's God en-
> dow you with a right to life and liberty. Then you
> have to keep the laws of God, for God's law is the
> only thing that gives you a right to be free.[36]

The search for freedom and individualism on the frontier thus culminated in the novels of Laura Ingalls Wilder

in the discovery of self-discipline. The entire web of controls—over nature, economic affairs, other people, and oneself—Wilder saw as interconnected. Whatever freedom and liberty the townspeople could establish could only exist in a society heavily governed by values, norms, and rules that established limits for their actions. Individualism was not the opposite of community but its analogue. Control did not preclude freedom; rightly understood, it established the foundation upon which freedom rested.

4 / Love and Affection in Wilder's Life and Writing

Laura Ingalls Wilder's novels are more than simply children's stories, more than a history of the frontier experience, more than one woman's autobiography. They are also—and this characteristic ranks highest in the minds of many readers—a first class love story. After returning from an October 1937 Book Week speech in Detroit, Wilder wrote to Lane that what the children there had wanted to learn first of all was how she and Almanzo had met and about their getting married.[1]

The entire series, in a way, is preparation for and a buildup to Laura's marriage to Almanzo, which takes place in the very last chapter of *These Happy Golden Years*. At the time of her Book Week speech Wilder was working on the novel that described her family's move to Dakota Territory when she was twelve years old and just entering adolescence. But by then she had clearly in mind the culmination of her multivolume novel, which, she informed her audience, "ends happily (as all good novels should) when Laura of the *Little Houses* and Almanzo of *Farmer Boy* were married."[2]

By the time she got married, Laura wasn't a little girl any longer, and although it is conceivable that Wilder could have continued her story into adulthood, that would have altered the nature of the entire series. Thus, it was not that when she finished the last of her eight installments in 1943 she was too tired of writing (although she must have been) or too old (seventy-six) to continue, but rather that the marriage to Almanzo marked the end of

Almanzo Wilder at the time he was courting Laura Ingalls. *(Courtesy Laura Ingalls Wilder-Rose Wilder Lane Museum and Home, Mansfield, Missouri)*

Laura's childhood and thus provided a logical culmination to this series of children's books. *The First Four Years*, an experiment that may have been written sometime in the thirties and was intended for a more adult audience, exposes the difficulty Wilder faced in trying to shift her point of view from that of a young girl and in attempting to treat more adult themes in her writing.[3] The book simply fails to resonate with its readers in the same way that the children's stories do, just as many marriages lose the romance that characterized the courtships leading up to them.

There is thus a natural direction to the love story that runs through the children's books, one that is clearly discernable, in retrospect, in the last two or three in the series. Laura's marriage to Almanzo seems fitting and proper—flowing directly out of all that has gone before. Not only do the two appear to be the perfect happy couple, but it is hard for readers to imagine either one in love with or married to anybody else. Partly this reaction derives from the romantic notions readers bring to their reading of the books; partly it emanates from cues the books themselves provide. Moonlight rides and romantic song lyrics heighten the feeling. "Sing the starlight song," Almanzo asks Laura on one of their buggy rides, and she sings it softly to him.

> In the starlight, in the starlight,
> At the daylight's dewy close,
> When the nightingale is singing
> His last love song to the rose;
> In the calm clear night of summer
> When the breezes softly play,
> From the glitter of our dwelling
> We will softly steal away.
> Where the silv'ry waters murmur
> By the margin of the sea,
> In the starlight, in the starlight,
> We will wander gay and free.[4]

The personality traits that emerged in Laura during childhood and adolescence developed within the familial context. Along with her mother and father and siblings, an extended kin network provided crucial determinants in the development of her sense of self. It was within a warm and loving but not always smoothly comfortable environment that Laura's sense of identity emerged as a child and solidified as an adolescent. Although she loved, admired, and respected her mother, Laura seemed to identify in many ways more closely with her father, especially with his wanderlust and desire to be free of the bonds of conventionality.[5] To underline the point, Laura frequently contrasted her own personality with that of Mary, whom she identified with her mother in her conventionally conservative approach to life.

Caution is necessary in drawing these conclusions because Laura exaggerated and simplified events and characters in order to enhance the narrative. The messy complications of everyday life that contribute to its complexity and paradox were frequently forgotten or transmuted in composing the books. A good example of this is the episode where Laura begs Ma to let her help Pa with haying in the fields. In real life, her mother sometimes actually joined in the work herself, but in her daughter's fictionalized accounts Ma was cast in the traditional role of a native-born middleclass white woman who was disturbed by the idea of women working in the fields.[6] Likewise, Laura's fictional aversion to sewing—a ladylike activity—belies the fact that in real life she enjoyed that occupation.[7]

Whatever the discrepancies between the fictional Laura and the real life Laura, the latter did forge her identity within the context of family life and the broader confines of late-nineteenth-century culture as it was manifested in a little railroad town on the edge of the agricultural frontier. The loving relationships that prevailed within the Ingalls household were not universally present, as Wilder well knew, and she described several decidedly different sorts of families in her books. The most memorable example of a dysfunctional family was the Brewsters, with whom she lived in their homestead shanty twelve miles south of town while she taught school in January, February, and March of 1883. In addition to her worries about discipline, Laura found the reception given her by Mrs. Brewster—"Lib"—cold and hostile. From Laura's description of her, Lib Brewster seems to have been a classic example of a homesteader wife dragged out to the frontier by her husband against her will and totally unable to adjust. Homicidal and suicidal, Mrs. Brewster threatens her husband with a knife in one memorable scene and continues to mistreat Laura and their son John the whole time Laura stayed with them.[8]

This was only one of several instances in the books where Wilder changed the names of her characters, perhaps fearing to embarrass a family. The Brewsters were actually the Bouchies, and the fictional Brewster school was the Bouchie school. Mr. Bouchie was a friend and distant relative of Robert Boast, who had arranged Laura's interview with the school superintendent for the job.[9] An item in the De Smet *Leader* the following year related a tragic story about the death of an Isaac Bouchie, who may or may not have been related to the Bouchies Laura was talking about. It did, however, provide a good example of the kind of unhappy relationships that could exist in a frontier home like the one Wilder described.

The death of Isaac Bouchie, notice of which is published elsewhere, was the tragic result of a family quarrel concerning which there are many and conflicting stories, making it impossible to arrive at the exact truth, and causing judgment to be generally suspended. A coroner's jury was called, and after a full investigation rendered a verdict in substance as follows:

"Isaac Bouchie came to his death by result of a wound on the cheek willfully and feloniously made by a large bone thrown by Clarence Bouchie instigated and abetted by his mother, Elizabeth Bouchie."

Elizabeth Bouchie was the step-mother of the deceased, and Clarence was his half-brother—a boy about thirteen years old. It appears that there was much unpleasantness between the boys, with probable blame on both sides, and that on the occasion in question the mother took a hand in the quarrel, with the result announced in the coroner's verdict. Mother and son were arraigned before Justice Owen, waived examination, and were released on bond of $500. The affair is a singular and complicated one, in which it will be very difficult to find the exact truth.[10]

Most family quarrels did not go that far, but serious conflict and bitterness were not uncommon. Not every family resembled the affectionate and mutually helpful model presented by the Ingallses. When Laura worked in town making shirts for Mr. Clancy (his real name was Clayson), she hated the yelling and the quarreling that went on among the children, the bickering between him and his mother-in-law, and the swearing. Once at the dinner table Laura "was so upset that she could not eat, she wanted only to get away." Then when things quieted down and bygones seemed to be bygones, Laura remembered her mother's saying, "It takes all kinds of people to make a world."[11]

"All kinds" included neighbor children Jennie and Gaylord Ross, who were nasty and mean to Laura and told dirty stories that she couldn't understand.[12] They also included George Masters and his young bride Maggie and their baby, who lived with the Ingalls family in Pa's store building in town during the hard winter of 1880-1881. Although Wilder included them in her initial autobiographical reminiscence "Pioneer Girl," these neighbors were omitted from The Long Winter, partly because in her eyes they were such unpleasant people.[13] More often, however, Wilder's neighbors were likable and admirable, like Mrs. McKee, who took Laura with her to "sit" a homestead north of Manchester; the Woodworths, who lived in the second-floor living quarters above the depot; and especially the Boasts, who were childless but always full of vim and vigor.[14]

On a scale of one to ten, the Ingalls family would have ranked near the top in the degree of love and affection that pervaded the household. In fact, Wilder's description of her family may seem almost too good to be true, and the reader suspects that some quarreling and unpleasantness must have been left out of the story. If anyone in the family was ever grouchy or unhelpful, it was usually Laura herself. For the most part, both parents and children were loving and affectionate and enjoyed doing household tasks together, singing, playing, and listening to stories and to Pa play his fiddle.

These shared activities helped the girls develop a secure sense of identity as they were growing up. But almost as soon as the foundations of selfhood were laid, the girls entered into another sort of game: relations with the opposite sex, a process that eventually would lead to their splitting off and forming their own families.

The dewy path to marriage described in the novels mirrored expectations late-nineteenth-century Americans had for themselves. Accompanying this idea was an increasingly clear-cut division in sex roles between the male, who was expected to be the breadwinner and to represent the family in the public arena, and the female, whose ultimate goal in life, it was widely accepted, was to become a homemaker and to raise children. If men were ruled by a success ethic that demanded hard work and promised pecuniary rewards and recognition for diligence and striving, women were elevated on a pedestal that denied them effective power but attributed to them superior moral virtue and qualities of piety, purity, domesticity, and submisssiveness. The separation of spheres that prevailed almost everywhere made the virtues ascribed to either sex almost opposite in nature. In contrast to women, men were expected to be self-controlled, courageous, aggressive, and independent. Yet after the Civil War, sex roles were no longer static or absolute but had become fluid and variable. By the late 1800s men increasingly were seen as "having heart," although they still were generally expected to hide their emotions in public.[15]

The values, implicit and explicit, embodied in the Little House books reflected dominant cultural themes of the period, but with a twist. Laura Ingalls and Almanzo Wilder both accepted the desirability of marriage as a matter of course and willingly took on the roles expected of them, for the most part. But without challenging the prevailing stereotypes frontally, Laura insisted on a degree of freedom for herself that made her something of a proto-feminist. As her life progressed in Dakota, and later in Missouri, Laura displayed more imagination and independence in charting out a path for herself as a married woman than did most of her female counterparts. If her self-described personality in the novels is at all accurate, we should not be surprised that she wound up iconoclastic. The very fact that she wrote the novels attests to that side of her personality.

The notion that romance should be the primary factor in choosing a mate was a relatively new one, having firmly established itself only during the late eighteenth and early nineteenth centuries in Europe and the United States.[16] New sexual stereotypes emerged simultaneously, limiting women to a passive, powerless role and investing men with initiative, power, and decision-making authority. Historians attribute the "separation of spheres," which hardened during the early 1800s, to economic and demographic changes that accompanied the rise of industrialism and the growth of urbanization. The role expectations defined by the culture of the time were plainly visible to Wilder as she was growing up and were clearly embodied in her mother's behavior. But, as Wilder described herself in her books, she frequently resisted the expectations that bore down upon her and opted instead for following her own inclinations and impulses. Therefore, if she wanted to help Pa working in the fields, she requested that she be allowed to do so. If she wanted to play ball with the boys at school, she did that too.[17]

There were limits to her iconoclasm, however. Most of her rebelliousness was relatively innocent and, from our point of view, perfectly understandable. She may have loosened her corset, but she didn't throw it away. For the most part, she was willing to follow the conventions of ordinary society. And when Almanzo, surprised at her insistence on omitting the word "obey" from their wedding ceremony, asked her if she was in favor of women's rights, she insisted that she was not. "I do not want to vote," she said. "But I can not make a promise that I will not keep, and, Almanzo, even if I tried, I do not think I could obey anybody against my better judgment."[18] Almanzo assured her that he would never expect her to; in fact, he said, any objective observer would have to agree that it would be morally reprehensible for anyone to do so.

For all her independence and rebelliousness, Laura was part and parcel of the culture of her time, expecting to fall in love and marry her ideal man and to raise a family. Sometimes she worried that she might lack the necessary qualifications, intimating that she would probably grow up to be an old maid. Laura's description of herself in "Pioneer Girl" as a roly-poly girl who could only afford to wear poor clothes contrasts sharply with her description of Nellie Oleson, who was tall, thin, light complexioned, and always wore nice clothes. Again, the reader must allow for some exaggeration, since Wilder's stories are fiction, after all, not simple autobiography. However, pictures of Wilder and her sisters taken at the time show her to have been a very pretty girl when she was in her teens—prettier than her sisters—and may help explain why she got married at eighteen and Grace and Carrie didn't marry until they were twenty-four and forty-one, respectively (Mary's blindness precluded her from trying to marry).[19]

The two main variables, besides one's own attributes, in the drama of pairing up with a future marriage partner are the pool of prospective mates and the competition that exists for them. In both instances, the novels tell a simpler story than evidently was true. It is clear that for narrative purposes Wilder simplified and rearranged the facts in telling the story. In the original "Pioneer Girl" manuscript, the first time Laura set eyes on Almanzo was when she and Carrie got lost in the slough by their homestead in 1881. In *The Long Winter*, the same episode is presented as happening in the fall of 1880.[20] In *Little Town on the Prairie*, Laura and Almanzo formally introduce themselves to each other right after she picks up her new name cards at Jake Hopp's newspaper office in the fall of 1881 and Almanzo offers to give her a ride over to the school. Incredibly, in "Pioneer Girl," it is not until a Sunday afternoon a year later when he takes her out sleighing—after he has escorted her home several times from revival services and transported her back and forth to the Bouchie school for eight weeks—that they finally get around to inquiring about each other's first names.[21]

Perhaps Wilder was a bit uncomfortable writing about a fourteen- or fifteen-year-old girl taking up with a man ten years older than she. Or perhaps she reduced Almanzo's fictional age by several years in order to enhance the plot line. Although he was actually twenty-two in 1879 when he and his brother Royal came out to Dakota Territory to find homesteads, Wilder described him in *The Long Winter* as nineteen—too young under the terms of the law to make a claim, which meant he had to lie about his age. Earlier, in writing "Pioneer Girl," she had lowered his age another two years to seventeen, which still would have made him five years older than she was.[22]

Wilder apparently was somewhat uncomfortable with the notion of child brides. The story in "Pioneer Girl" of the shotgun wedding of George and Maggie Masters didn't get into the finished novels, but another story about a thirteen-year-old child bride was included in *By the Shores of Silver Lake*. Laura and her cousin Lena, twelve and thirteen at the time, were both glad they did not have to worry about such a prospect because they did not want to lose their freedom that way. In a letter to her daughter in 1938, Wilder indicated her concern that readers might think her too young to have married and judge it a "horrid child marriage."[23]

Another alteration Wilder made to the truth is the number of suitors she had during her teenage years. In "Pioneer Girl," Wilder treated humorously the case of Alfred Thomas, a young lawyer in De Smet who came to visit one evening and asked her *parents* if they were planning to go to an entertainment; he was too timid to invite Laura directly to go with him, so she missed a chance to have an escort. Later a young man named Arthur Johnson took Laura home from church one evening when Almanzo wasn't there. Then there was the week, mentioned in *These Happy Golden Years*, that Laura got three different invitations to go out. "I declare," Ma said, "it never rains but it pours." These suitors Wilder left faceless and anonymous.[24]

The courtship of one boy, however, she described in detail. Ernest Perry, a farm youth who lived on a farm a mile south of the Ingalls place, took such a liking to Laura that he waited years to marry after she rejected him. He was a big strong lad who once walked in his bare feet to plow some of Pa's land. When Ernie asked Laura to go to a party with him at one of the neighboring farm homes, she was glad to accept the invitation and enjoyed herself, even though she felt awkward at square dancing and didn't like the kissing games. The second time she went with him, however, she disliked the crowd and the kissing games even more, and when her "date" tried to put his arm around her on the way home, she decided not to go out with him again. Another young man, who hired himself out to the Wilder brothers and often ran around with them, was described by Laura in "Pioneer Girl" as "a romantic figure." He was Oscar Rhuel, a Swedish immigrant who had come to America in pursuit of a girl he had been engaged to back home before she was carted off by her parents to California. He eventually managed to catch up with her there and marry her. Wilder wrote that "we girls felt a great sympathy for him, and I thought him quite handsome," but he apparently had no romantic interest in her.[25]

The one person besides Almanzo whom Laura seems to have taken a particular interest in was Edward Garland, known to everyone as "Cap." Cap, who was about Laura's age, lived with his mother at her boarding house on the lot back of the Ingalls store on Second Street. When the Ingallses were living in town, Laura must have seen a lot of him, since their backyards adjoined each other and the Garlands would have walked up Second Street past the In-

Looking southwest from the courthouse around 1900. The old Ingalls store building is in the center of the picture to the left of the circular bandstand, and the two-story 1884 school building is visible on the horizon. *(Courtesy South Dakota State Historical Society)*

galls building every time they went to school or church or had business on Main Street. Cap was the first student Laura noticed the first time she and Carrie walked to school, and that chapter—"Cap Garland"—is one of only three in the series named for an individual.[26]

Laura was apprehensive as she and Carrie first approached the schoolhouse, but then she saw one of the boys leaping through the air to catch a ball. "He was tall and quick and he moved as beautifully as a cat. His yellow hair was sun-bleached almost white and his eyes were blue. They saw Laura and opened wide. Then a flashing grin lighted up his whole face and he threw the ball to her." Laura's reflexive reaction was to jump and catch the ball, but then some other boys yelled, "Girls don't play ball!" and Laura threw the ball back, saying that she really didn't want to play. This chapter, which begins with Cap encouraging Laura to break out of her stereotypical gender role, ends with the students and their teacher braving the wintry blasts of the year's first snowstorm to get home safely, with Cap trudging off alone on his own path—ever the individualist and nonconformist.[27]

Either consciously or unconsciously, Laura seems to have regarded Cap as the analogue of her own dreams of freedom and independence. She saw in him a free spirit, willing to buck convention. And besides—that golden hair and those blue eyes! Was Cap Laura's romantic ideal? Did she perhaps see many of her own personality traits mirrored in him? It is interesting that Almanzo shared some of Cap's finer qualities, most notably his bravery, and that he and Cap became best friends later, even though Almanzo was about a decade older. It was Cap and Almanzo who risked their lives during the hard winter to go out and get wheat from the farmer in the countryside to save the town from starvation. Cap did it for no other evident motive than altruism; Almanzo did it so that he could save his own seed wheat for spring planting.

Cap, if we can rely on the books, seems not to have had any particular romantic interest in Laura. Indeed, it was he who challenged Almanzo to pick Laura up at the Brewster school on a particularly cold Friday in February 1883 and take her home to her parents for the weekend.[28] But apparently the reciprocal was not true, for Laura did, at least for a fleeting moment, have romantic designs on Cap. In fact, at the revival meeting where Almanzo first asked to walk her home, it was Cap that Laura had had her eye on, not Almanzo. This preference came through more clearly in Wilder's original description of the episode in her "Pioneer Girl" manuscript than it did in *Little Town on the Prairie*. Almanzo, Cap, and Oscar Rhuel were all at the revival meeting, Laura wrote in the original version, and "to be perfectly truthful I was noticing Cap." In the novel, Cap plays only a peripheral role. As Laura and Almanzo walked across the snow-covered ground between the church and her home, neither could think of anything to say. "She wished that Mr. Wilder would say something. A faint scent of cigar smoke came from his thick overcoat. It was pleasant, but not as homelike as the scent of Pa's pipe. It was a more dashing scent, it made her think of

Cap and this young man daring that dangerous trip to bring back the wheat."[29]

But several walks home from revival meetings do not a courtship make. Laura was pleased by the attention Almanzo gave her, although not entirely sure how to respond to it. Some weeks later, when he drove out to pick her up in the country from her schoolteaching job, she was embarrassed when the students started referring to Almanzo as "teacher's beau." She resolved to straighten the matter out and to let him know that while she accepted his kindness with gratitude, she felt under no obligation to him and did not expect to keep seeing him after her job was done. "He was so much older; he was a homesteader," she thought. "The truth is that when I came back from Bouchie's I had rather hoped to leave Manly [Almanzo] and go with Cap," Wilder wrote in "Pioneer Girl." But at the next opportunity—when she saw all of her friends out sleighing with their beaus on a wintry Sunday afternoon—she immediately responded with a hearty "Oh, yes!" to Almanzo's invitation to go sleighing with him. Almanzo revealed his own insight into psychology when he replied, "I thought maybe you'd change your mind after you watched the crowd go by." Almanzo's calculations were certainly correct, for as they rode around in his cutter, Laura was "so happy that she had to sing."[30]

In her original "Pioneer Girl" manuscript, Wilder wrote that before Almanzo invited her to ride with him, she had been looking out the window, wishing that she could join in the fun. "Mary Power and Cap Garland went by in a cutter built for two. I hadn't seen Cap for a long time. He might have taken me this once, I thought." That reference to Cap gets toned down in *These Happy Golden Years* to "the full music of double strings of bells came swiftly, and Mary Power and Cap Garland dashed by in a cutter. So that was what Mary was doing. Cap Garland had a cutter and full strings of sleigh bells, too." Thus, Laura's original wish that Cap would invite her to ride with him got written out of the story. In a revised version of "Pioneer Girl" that was sent to agent Carl Brandt, the episode is described simply as "Mary Power and Cap Garland went by in a cutter made for two. I hadn't seen Cap for a long time." In a second revision, which was sent to agent George Bye, the second sentence about not seeing Cap for a long time was excised.[31]

The sleighing episode was the turning point in Laura and Almanzo's relationship (at least in its fictional guise), and after that the burden was as much on Laura to "keep her man" as it was on Almanzo to "make his catch." The story was not a simple progression to the altar, by any means. There was work to do and school to be taught and life to be lived. More than two years would pass before sleigh bells were transformed into wedding bells. In the meantime, Laura was concerned that somebody else— perhaps prettier and more alluring than she—might steal Almanzo away from her. We cannot re-create what actually went on in the hearts and minds of the romantic duo during this period of time. It is certain, however, that the story of Laura's competitors for Almanzo's affection was more complicated than the way she told it, just as the story of her own batch of suitors was more complex than the one she recorded.

The villain in the books is Nellie Oleson—tall, lovely complexioned, and beautiful but also vain, manipulative, and overbearing. To endow the telling of the story with dramatic unity, Wilder combined in the persona of Nellie Oleson three different girls—Nellie Owens, whom she had known back in Walnut Grove, where Nellie's father had been a storekeeper; Genevieve Masters, another former Walnut Grove girl, whose father Sam Masters had been a schoolteacher and later had a homestead west of De Smet; and Stella Gilbert, who lived on a farm northeast of town.[32]

Despite the similarity of the names Nellie Owens and Nellie Oleson, the fictional character was actually modeled more upon Genevieve Masters, who, as Wilder wrote in "Pioneer Girl," "had grown tall and slim; she had a beautiful complexion and was always very nicely dressed," a description almost identical to the one given

Nellie Oleson in *Little Town on the Prairie*. Stella Gilbert was rather an innocent victim, whose mother was bedridden and who Almanzo thought needed somebody to bring a little cheerfulness into her life. That is why, according to "Pioneer Girl," he took her on several Sunday afternoon buggy rides around the countryside with him and Laura. Stella fit Laura's narrative purposes neatly, for by folding her character into that of Nellie Oleson, she could be seen trying to manipulate Almanzo and lure him away from Laura (which, in fact, Stella may well have been trying to do).[33] Probably Laura simply disliked girls like Nellie Owens and Genevieve Masters because they fit all the stereotypical descriptions of pampered beauties who disdained active outdoor types like herself and played up to all of men's foolish inclinations.

Yet, in the end Laura won out in the struggle for Almanzo's affections. Why? Largely because she successfully played the culturally prescribed role of a young maiden—and she liked his horses! Love, after all, is not a simple unmediated emotion or unrefined biological urge. Rather, it is, in a real sense, a social construction—a set of feelings, thoughts, and actions that people are supposed to and expected to experience under the appropriate circumstances. Robert C. Solomon reminds us that

> what we call "love" is not a universal phenomenon but a culture-specific interpretation of the universal phenomenon of sexual attraction and its complications. Love may begin in biology, but it is essentially a set of ideas that may even turn against the biological impulses that are at their source. The history of romantic love is the history of a special set of attitudes toward sex, even where sex is never mentioned.[34]

Laura consciously refused to acknowledge any role that sex might play. She wrote her daughter in 1938, contrasting the conditions of young people then with the situation in her own day, that it had been almost a different civilization back then. There had been no question of sex for young adolescents—they had never even thought of it. "Put sex and all relating to it out of your mind," she wrote.[35] But since Freud, at least, we know that what you see is not necessarily what you get—what one is conscious of is not necessarily what impels him or her to act. Laura must have experienced sexual attraction, but like most of her fellow Victorians, she was unwilling to admit it. She played the role that was given to her as she saw it. Her parents, her religion, her friends, and everything she had learned in school drove her to behave in prescribed ways, which she deemed fit and proper. When Almanzo tried to slip his arm over her shoulder on a buggy ride, she leaned forward and spurred the horses on so he would have to take over the reins. Almanzo did not dare try to kiss her, even on the evening she said she would marry him. "Aren't you going to kiss me good night?" she asked him when he dropped her off at her house. "I was afraid you wouldn't like it," he replied honestly.[36]

In sending Lane her proposed outline for what later became *These Happy Golden Years*, Wilder described the indirect nature of Almanzo's marriage proposal and her response to it.

"Do you want an engagement ring?"
"That would depend on who gave it to me."
"If I should give it to you?"
"Then it would depend on the ring."

Laura's comment on her response: "Fact! This was Manly's proposal and my answer. It was what you might call laconic and illustrates something about us at that time and place I have tried to express."[37]

But after a trip back home to Minnesota in late 1884, Almanzo showed up on the Ingalls doorstep on Christmas Eve and he and Laura kissed each other in front of all the folks.[38] That was a sign of their love and an appropriate public expression of it. Throughout their relationship with each other, the couple had played two different roles with each other—one in public, one in private—but both were firmly grounded in the expectations and prescriptions embedded in Victorian culture. Although Laura may have deviated somewhat from role expectations in her flights of imagination and assertions of independence, for the most part she, too, comfortably acquiesced in the roles defined for her by society.

The love story that runs through the Wilder books tells us much about both the personal lives of Laura and her family and the kinds of relations that existed between men and women on the frontier in the late nineteenth century. Her books are biography, but they are history, too. Wilder acknowledges the romantic love that exists between a man and a woman, but her description of the kind of love that makes homes joyful places, rather than nightmares of rancor and discord, is one of the main benefits we readers derive from reading her books.

5 / Fact and Interpretation in Wilder's Fiction

In recent years Charles Sanders Peirce (1839–1914) has come to be recognized as one of America's geniuses—a wide-ranging polymath who ranks as perhaps our foremost philosopher and a major contributor in a number of fields of inquiry, from physics and chemistry to psychology and the history of science. His semiotic theory (he preferred the spelling "semeiotic")—or "science of signs"—can be applied fruitfully to the interpretation of literature. At the core of Peirce's formulation is the notion of the "sign," which he said "is something which stands to somebody for something in some respect or capacity." Signs have an apparently infinite capacity for generating other signs, which enable individuals to whom the signs are addressed to interpret their world around them. For our purposes, the kind of sign that is of interest is the "interpretant," which serves to interpret or give meaning to other signs, that is, to the perceptible world around us. Semiotics (or semiotic theory) thus is preeminently a matter of interpreting everyday experience.[1]

In this chapter, I want to show how in Wilder's popular children's books these interpretants emerged within the context of the society and culture in which she lived. Interpretation does not occur in a vacuum but is influenced by and limited by what Peirce called "collateral experi-

A shorter version of this chapter appears in John Deely and Terry Prewitt, eds., *Semiotics 1991* (Lanham, Md.: University Press of America, 1993), pp. 158–64.

ence," or "collateral observation," which encompasses all of the knowledge, experience, and mental baggage that incline a particular interpreter, such as Wilder, in a particular instance to choose one possible interpretant over another. It is important to investigate the contexts in which semiosis—or sign action—occurs, for only through increasing our understanding of such contexts can we adequately explain how, in fact, particular interpretants come to the fore in particular places and times.[2]

The novels, when set in historical context, reveal a complex process of perception, interpretation, and recall occurring in Wilder's art. These activities are never simple, of course. Everything we perceive is mediated through a variety of filters—our knowledge, background, circumstances, desires, feelings, assumptions, institutional affiliations, class, status, gender, age, and so forth. We tend to see what we want to see, to remember what we are predisposed to remember. We strive to make sense of our world, to interpret it as best we can. In our quest for meaning and understanding, we choose from a smorgasbord of interpretants—links between signs and objects that enable us to make sense of the world we inhabit.

My purpose here is to discover how interpretation occurred—in Peirce's terms, how "interpretants" operated to establish meaning for Laura first of all as the character she later wrote about in the novels and then later in the actual writing process. Although her vocabulary diverged from Peirce's, who said that "all this universe is perfused with signs," I think she would have understood what he meant by it.[3] For Wilder, the world was perfused with meaning; objects did not stand starkly in isolation from each other but, rather, were linked in webs of significance based on interpersonal relationships in family, school, church, community, work, play, courtship, ritual, and a hundred other ways. Meaning was not arbitrary or amenable to individual whim but was established within certain parameters by tradition, practice, authority, prescription, and common expectation.

The Little Town novels illustrate how interpretants

came "ready made," so to speak, to Wilder as she confronted her world of signs. My focus here is on institutions, gossip and informal community pressure, the media, stories, slogans and wise sayings, songs, roles, and certain kinds of oppositions that imparted meaning and significance into what might otherwise have remained meaningless phenomena. All of these operated as templates or organizing devices for interpretation and limiting choices, thus making people's thinking more predictable and consistent than it otherwise would have been.

The image of the frontier as a land of savagery is belied by the panoply of civilizing influences and institutions that quickly established themselves in railroad towns like De Smet. As soon as the construction of the Chicago and North Western Railroad was completed in 1880, a rush of settlers arrived and towns began springing up all along the line at regular intervals.[4] The accoutrements of civilization were hauled in on boxcar after boxcar: pictures, pianos, rugs, sofas, Bibles, poetry books, newspapers, wallpaper, suits of clothes, umbrellas, band uniforms, roller skates, farm machinery. Along with the things people carried with them or purchased in the stores on Main Street, they brought along attitudes, ideas, beliefs, feelings, prejudices, and habits. They quickly moved to establish the kinds of institutions they had been familiar with in Minnesota, Wisconsin, Iowa, Illinois, New York, and New England—churches, schools, literary societies, chicken pie suppers, singing schools, box socials, Odd Fellows lodges, and women's study circles.[5] The institutional matrix within which the settlers lived provided ready-made definitions and prescriptions and thus channeling their thought and behavior. Clear limits existed on the interpretations a girl in her early teens could give to the world she saw around her.

The family, the central social institution in a town like De Smet, taught Laura the roles she was expected to play in life—daughter, student, schoolteacher, belle, housewife, mother. As a dutiful daughter, she learned to do all of the things a young girl was expected to do—cook,

clean, wash, sew, tend the garden, take care of her younger sisters, and obey her parents. Although she displayed
considerable independence of mind as she was growing
up, Laura fit easily into the role of starry-eyed maiden, in-
viting approaches from young men whose intentions were
marriage. In many ways, the overarching influence of family ties imposed itself on Laura's thinking and actions.

At school Laura and the other children memorized
songs, poems, even history, all of which were designed to
instill certain values and habits of thought in them. Slogans and maxims learned at school were often reinforced
by hearing them repeated by adults at home or on the
street. Culture reinforced itself in a social-institutional
setting that was essentially homogeneous and harmoni-
ous. Certainly conflict and differences of opinion were not
absent, but people generally managed to negotiate com-
promises and maintain a large degree of social consensus.
School was as important for teaching promptness, good
behavior, good work habits, and cooperation as it was for
passing on the three R's.

Religion was the third major institution influencing
people's ideas and behavior. The first church service in
town was held in the Ingalls home. Ma and Pa helped organize the Congregational church in town, and Pa did
some of the carpentry work on the building. In the Ingalls
family everybody knew that Sunday was a day to go to
church and a day to rest. They took religion seriously but
were matter-of-fact about it, not like Mr. McKee, a strict
Presbyterian who believed in no laughing or smiling on
Sundays, just Bible reading and biblical lessons. Some of
Laura's and Almanzo's best memories were of the long
buggy rides they took on Sunday afternoons all over the
Dakota prairie. During the great blizzards of the hard winter, when nobody dared venture outside, the Ingalls girls
passed the time by doing Sunday School lessons, memorizing Bible verses, and singing hymns.[6]

Not all channeling of people's behavior occurred within
formal institutional settings. Gossip and informal community pressure, which exerted their influence in a vari-

ety of ways, were crucial to the process of social control in a town like De Smet. When Daniel Loftus tried to profit from the starving conditions confronting the settlers during the long winter (see Chapter 3), he was in some eyes merely following accepted business practice. But that's not the way most of the people in town saw it at the time, and they forced him to back down.[7] In the confrontation between Loftus and the townspeople, two alternative interpretations competed for dominance: the first an individualistic one based on capitalistic, competitive assumptions; the second a communal one based on the needs of the collective whole. In this instance, social pressure carried the day.

A third sort of interpretive template operating in Wilder's novels related to the increasing importance of mass media in American life. The manifestations in De Smet during the late nineteenth century of what amounted to a communications revolution were much less obvious than they were in places like Omaha or Chicago, but they were present nonetheless. Pa Ingalls subscribed to the Chicago *Interocean* and the St. Paul *Pioneer Press*, both of which had local tie-ins with the De Smet *Leader* for reduced subscription rates.[8] Thus, De Smetites could read the same kind of national and international news that residents of hundreds of similar little railroad towns were reading all over Dakota Territory and the entire United States. Ma Ingalls subscribed to *Advance*, a church women's magazine, and the girls read *Youth's Companion*.[9] Thus, although the influence of the mass media was much smaller than it would become during the next several decades when movies, radio, and eventually television made their appearance, the media were already beginning to influence and homogenize the ideas and thoughts of De Smet's citizens during the 1880s.

More important to De Smetites than the media, which received little mention in Wilder's novels, were the stories that were told and retold. Pa had a gift for storytelling, something Laura apparently picked up from him.[10] She certainly heard many stories, if her books are to be believed, and her novels, in a way, are one long retelling of the stories she heard as a girl and lived and experienced as she was growing up. Stories were told not only to describe things but to explain them—both to the listeners and to the storyteller. Wilder seemed to believe that if the raw materials of daily experience could be shaped into narrative form, they would have meaning for people. Not that she said so in so many words, but this notion runs like a bright thread through all of her writings. Storytelling was a way of making sense of the world, providing enjoyable moments of leisure away from work, reassuring people in time of danger, and instilling hope for the future and inspiration for going on and making the best of life.

Commonly repeated slogans also pointed up morals or wisdom for people to live by, and Laura learned her lessons well, for she accumulated a repertoire of slogans or wise sayings which she called upon on many occasions. Her books are full of people applying such folk wisdom to every aspect of their lives. "All's well that ends well," Ma said when Pa got home safely from his trip to the land office to file on the homestead, and Laura repeated the same thing when she and Carrie found Pa in the hayfield after they had been temporarily lost in the big slough.[11] Such slogans provided reassurance, guidance, and comfort and gave meaning to lives buffeted by a variety of environmental, social, and economic threats and challenges. Thus, Ma felt better when she said, "There's no great loss without some small gain," after baking a pie made from the blackbirds that had eaten the corn crop. Similarly, "Pride goes before a fall," she observed after a foolhardy railroad superintendent from the East tried to ram a locomotive through a blockade of snow and ice on the tracks, and "The Lord helps them that help themselves," Laura reassured Mary, who was fretting that she would never get to college.[12]

"Where there's a will there's a way," "A body makes his own luck, be it good or bad," "We must cut our coat to fit the cloth," and "Gather ye roses while ye may" were all slogans that reinforced community norms and social expectations, undergirded values, promoted striving and work, and cemented morale. They were believed and accepted precisely because they were not called into question, and repetition made them secure. Yet, at intervals doubts might spring up regarding some of them, as when Ma caught herself arguing against her own slogan, "Married in black, you'll wish yourself back." When Laura cheerfully replied that even though she'd be wearing black, she'd also be wearing her sage-green poke bonnet with blue silk lining, Ma allowed, "I don't suppose there's any truth in these old sayings."[13] Yet if people had not found any truth in them, they wouldn't have repeated the sayings as often as they did. That Laura assumed their importance for explaining the lives of people is clear from her frequent inclusion of them in her books. They were taken for granted as an element of everyday life.

So were songs, which served as another template for organizing people's feelings and thoughts. Wilder's books are full of songs and fragments of songs. She was able to recall from memory dozens of the old songs her family had sung around the fireplace or kitchen table as Pa played merrily on his fiddle. Singing was the most memorable part of their family ritual for her. The very last words Wilder wrote for publication in the series were two lines from a song at the end of *These Happy Golden Years*: "Golden Years are passing by, These happy, golden years."[14]

Although many of the songs she included were happy, a few were sad. Songs, indeed, were a way of capturing feeling and emotion, and they were a way of regulating people's emotional lives and training them in what kinds of emotions were permissible, what kinds were desirable, and by their absence, what kinds should be suppressed. During the hardships of the long winter, Pa would sing his "trouble song," slapping his arms on his chest:

Oh, I am as happy as a big sunflower (Slap! Slap)
That nods and bends in the breezes, Oh! (Slap! Slap!)
And my heart (Slap!) is as light (Slap!) as the wind

that blows (Slap! Slap!)
The leaves from off the trees, Oh! (Slap! SLAP!)[15]

A clear case of denial, a Freudian would say. The wind is shrieking outside, the fuel is gone so hay has to be tied into tight bundles to burn in the stove, food supplies are low, and there is nothing to do but sit and wait out the blizzard. How to react? A realistic assessment of the desperate situation could only lead to gloom and depression; Pa's trouble song was an antidote with a useful result, a means of channeling his emotions along positive lines. If nothing else, the slapping of his hands was one way to keep them warm.

During the long winter, Ma, for her part, took Grace in her arms and, with Carrie crowded in the rocking chair beside her, rocked slowly and softly sang:

I will sing you a song of that beautiful land,
The far away home of the soul
Where no storms ever beat on that glittering strand
While the years of eternity roll.[16]

Songs and Pa's fiddle music were a regular part of Laura's family life, but they played a particularly important role at transition points in their lives—as when the family moved or when Laura married. At those times Pa would get out the fiddle, and they would have a sing. The songs the Ingallses sang were nostalgic as well as forward looking, happy, rambunctious, merry, wistful, romantic, hopeful. They helped shape the emotions of a girl and young woman in the same way they did for others in her society. Singing made Laura happy, which is probably why she did so much of it and made music and songs such an important part of her books.[17]

The roles that people were assigned also influenced the way they looked at their worlds, as the roles themselves dictated how they were expected to behave and instructed them in how to interpret things around them. A child's role was to defer to one's parents and other adults and to behave appropriately. Once, when Laura was falsely accused by a teacher of causing trouble in school, Pa and the other school board members visited the school to observe. That evening Laura did not bring the subject up until he did, wondering what he would say to her, for "it was not her place to speak of what had happened, until he did."[18]

But when Laura became a schoolteacher herself, she took on a new role. "She was a teacher now, and must act like one," but it was difficult at first for her to know how to perform. So when her students asked her to come out and throw snowballs, impulsively she did, until she remembered who she was. Then "she knew that she must not play any more. She was too small and too young; she would not be able to keep her pupils in order if she played games with them."[19] Her role, in other words, determined her behavior. When the school term was over and she returned to high school in De Smet, she could revert to her girlish behavior if she wanted, because then she would be playing the role of student, not teacher. Thus one's position and behavior in any situation was in large measure dictated by the expectations attached to the role the person was playing.

A final example of Wilder's method of interpretation is the way in which she cast phenomena and events into patterns of opposition. Through these oppositions we can discover how Wilder imbued her books with meaning. Charles Sanders Peirce, according to Michael Shapiro, identified opposition as the primary dyadic relation. "Indeed, for Peirce, 'a thing without oppositions *ipso facto* does not exist,' hence it is the study of oppositions which underlies the understanding of the mode of being of things."[20]

Many oppositions can be noted in Wilder's novels. In the first place, gender roles were well defined, reflecting the clear separation of spheres that existed in late-nineteenth-century America. However, ethnic identification did not play a major role in Wilder's novels; apparently ethnicity did not mean much to her. Now and then a reference to a Scandinavian farmwoman or an Irishman creeps in, but there is no sense of competition between natives and immigrants or among immigrant groups. There is only one ethnic conflict that figures prominently in Wilder's books—that between Indians and whites. Laura's Ma was scared of Indians, but Pa tried to understand them and sympathize with them. In her "Pioneer Girl" manuscript, Wilder alluded to anti-Catholic sentiment in De Smet, but those references were excluded from the published novels.[21]

What religious divisions there were in "the little town on the prairie," as presented in Wilder's novels, existed not between religious denominations but between churchgoers and nonchurchgoers or atheists. The Wilders and most of their friends did not wear religion on their sleeves, but they did not tolerate atheists; belief in God was a given and not to be questioned. Once when Laura suggested that she might stay home and study rather than attend a revival meeting, Nellie Oleson sounded horrified: "Why, people who don't go to revival meetings are *atheists*!" To her, and no doubt to Laura, too, the word atheist had the same connotations that "communist" would have later.[22]

Age groupings also separated people and helped determine their interpretations of things. Parents and children were clearly separated by work roles, authority, and responsibility. When children came of age and entered into the world of adulthood, boys were expected to go to work, and girls were expected to marry and have children. In the spring of 1881, as she turned fourteen, Laura realized that she "was too old now to play any more." All she could do was watch the boys play. In church, age divisions were also apparent: the "gray beards" sat up front, families in the middle, and boys in the back.[23]

Oppositions also delineated space. The treeless Dakota prairie presented an impressive sight to first visitors like the Ingallses when they arrived in 1879. Laura looked at the land and out to the horizon, which defined the boundary between prairie and sky. Sometimes she called the horizon the "edge of the sky," sometimes the "edge of the world," sometimes the "edge of the west." Both prairie and sky could be enhancing and alluring, both could be menacing and dangerous. The prairie was empty, quiet, treeless, but nevertheless magnificent, with the wind rustling through the grass and making it undulate like ocean waves. But the prairie also harbored wolves and other wild predators. Prairie fires raced across it, and the land itself could turn hostile and withhold its plenty (the theme of *The First Four Years*). The sky, likewise, was magnificently beautiful with its gorgeous sunsets and bright twinkling stars in the evening. But it, too, could destroy and sometimes did with fierce blizzards, hailstorms, and searing heat.[24]

If the prairie was set in opposition to the sky, the more important dualism in Laura's mind was between prairie countryside and the town. At first Laura was in love with the land and fearful of the people in town, which she perceived as a "sore" on the landscape—too dirty, too crowded, too lonely. She was scared there, not sure how to behave. As time went by, however, her mind changed and she decided she liked town living better, with all of its activities and with all of the people she had come to know. After marrying a farmer, she realized even more how difficult making a living from the land could be, and while she still enjoyed the land's beauty, she came to resent the meager rewards it offered for the hard labor put into it by her and her husband, Almanzo.[25]

The town itself was split, as so many were, between the proverbially good part of town and the end that lay "on the other side of the tracks." In De Smet most of the town huddled on the south side of the tracks. Laura referred to the part north of the tracks as "poverty flat," repeating what locals called it during the early years.[26] Besides this reference, though, there is very little evidence of class division in the Little House books. All the farmers were apparently in essentially similar situations, as were the storekeepers, the people who provided services, and so forth. This situation may partly reflect the democratic, all-in-it-together feeling that often exists during the early stages of community-building. But within a few years' time, the more successful residents begin to separate themselves from the less successful. Also, during her teen years, Wilder was less sophisticated and insightful than she would be later on about such distinctions of wealth and income and did not remark on them in her books. A historian would probably comment on the rise of the Farmers' Alliance and political protest during this period, but Wilder includes none of this in her account, which simply describes the struggle of one family trying to make a go of it under difficult conditions.

In Wilder's novels, the stories are meant to be history in the purest sense—faithful renderings of the adolescence and early adult years of a woman living on the agricultural frontier during the 1880s, and she does provide a useful account of frontier life as seen through the eyes of one person. The interpretations she gave to people, places, and things were heavily influenced by a set of templates provided her by her culture—institutions, gossip and informal community pressure, etc.—which influenced the interpretants she attached to the phenomena she perceived. A person growing up in the same circumstances would hardly have been able to think and act any differently. The interpretations she gave to her world were set within certain rather strict limits, but our knowledge of the historical circumstances surrounding these events helps us to place them into broader perspective. Only with the aid of such collateral information can we fully understand the attribution of meaning in her writing.

6 / Narrative Rules and the Process of Storytelling

Given a chance to comment on her own storytelling, Laura Ingalls Wilder's first impulse was to recall the stories she had heard her father tell as she and her sisters were growing up on the frontier. Her mother had taught them from books and trained them in manners, but her father had taught them other things and entertained them. "We had a busy happy childhood," Wilder told a Detroit Book Week audience in 1937, "but of it all, Sister Mary and I loved Pa's stories best. We never forgot them and I have always felt they were too good to be altogether lost."[1]

When her daughter Rose Wilder Lane finally persuaded her to sit down and record her own remembered stories of childhood, it quickly became apparent that transforming the raw materials of personal memory into a coherent, readable narrative would not be a simple task. Wilder's first attempt—her autobiographical "Pioneer Girl"—interested no publishers. Only after a painstaking process of reconceptualization, revision, and editorial intervention by Lane did Wilder find a publisher for her first novel, *Little House in the Big Woods*.[2]

In the process of writing eight novels (plus one published posthumously) Wilder steadily honed her craft and gained in her understanding of narrative technique, but until the very end she depended heavily upon Lane's editorial advice and revisions to complete and polish the manuscripts. Through it all, the mother-daughter team was guided by certain rules of storytelling, both explicit and implicit. Some of these guidelines got clear enunciation in letters that passed between them while their collaboration continued in *By the Shores of Silver Lake* and *The Long Winter*. Others can be inferred from a critical reading of the novels themselves and where drafts still exist, by examining their evolution into the finished products.

Stories played a variety of important roles in the Ingalls family while Laura and her sisters were growing up on the Wisconsin-Kansas-Minnesota-Iowa-Dakota frontier during the 1870s and 1880s. "There was no radio to amuse us then, no moving pictures to go to," Wilder recalled many years later, "so when the day's work was done, we sat in the twilight or by the evening lamp and listened to Pa's stories and the music of his violin."[3] Telling and reading stories became a well-entrenched family ritual, relieving boredom, providing enjoyment, and conjuring up old times. When blizzards blew during the long winter, Ma would read to the girls or Pa would tell them a story. They especially enjoyed listening to selections from *Youth's Companion* and from Pa's big green book, *The Wonders of the Animal World*. When Mary went off to college, Grace begged her to tell one last story before departing.[4] Beyond the confines of home, stories linked family members to the broader community. Bible stories learned in Sunday School reinforced lessons they had learned at home from Ma's reading of them.[5] Heroic stories about the Founding Fathers learned from history books at school found parallel expression in patriotic orations on the Fourth of July, since American history was, after all, one long story of bravery and progress.[6]

More than simply providing diversion and entertainment, stories did much to reduce the confusion and mystery of everyday life, rendering it consistent and meaningful. The function of narrative, David Carr contends, is to organize experience and render it coherent, thereby enabling people to make sense of it. But as Alasdair MacIntyre reminds us, "Stories are lived before they are told."[7] If they claim to be historically relevant, stories cannot be completely fabricated but must conform in some fashion to external events. Our versions of reality are bound to be, to some degree, constructed, rather than descriptions of external "reality." The extent to which they are constructed is a matter for critical judgment. In any event, stories constitute a major means of locating meaning in our lives.

In addition, stories help establish personal identity, for in transforming private experience into public discourse, they locate us within the larger community and help us define who we are. The ways in which people tell their stories—the particular kinds of language and narrative style upon which they rely—draw upon a storehouse of examples that are commonly repeated within communities. In the words of Peter Brooks, "Our lives are ceaselessly intertwined with narrative, with the stories that we tell and hear told, those we dream or imagine or would like to tell, all of which are reworked in that story of our own lives that we narrate to ourselves in an episodic, sometimes semi-conscious, but virtually uninterrupted monologue."[8]

One can detect a natural evolution in the stories related in Wilder's novels. The first several books revolve around stories Wilder had heard over and over again as a child. As the series progresses, Pa's stories become less frequent, and the narratives emerge out of the remembered experiences of Wilder herself, assimilated within her own style of storytelling. Her first rule in refashioning these stories into novel form was to tell them as accurately as possible—to make truthfulness the first criterion. Wilder strove diligently to get her facts right, making sure that the correct flowers were blooming on the prairie and the right songs were sung at church and recording accurately details like rates of interest at the bank, techniques of railroad construction, and the location of stores on Main Street. Because her books were autobiographical, invention was scarcely necessary, but autobiography carried a price with it. "Unfortunately we have used real names in these books and must stick closer to facts than otherwise we would need to do," Wilder wrote her daughter.[9] In order to recall these facts, Wilder relied primarily upon her ability to dredge up the past from her memory, but she also utilized artifacts she had saved, information from relatives and friends, and three visits back to De Smet—in 1931, 1938, and 1939.

Historical accuracy, however, was merely a necessary condition, not a guarantee of a good story, and Wilder was willing to sacrifice accuracy, if necessary, in order to promote the story line. For instance, a note she made on a draft of *The First Four Years*, which she never attempted to publish, referred to a scene in which Laura had taken a pitchfork in hand to confront some howling wolves. She commented, "All true except that I heard the last howl just before I went out and did not go but why spoil a good story for truth's sake."[10] Dates or names could be changed, ages modified, actions made up or reconstructed, and episodes created out of whole cloth. In reworking the stories for publication, Lane sometimes made up scenes that were within the spirit of the actions being described by her mother. Thus, although they are accurate in most respects, Wilder's novels cannot be regarded as actual history. They are fiction and responded to the dictates of that genre.

To streamline the narrative, many people who had been part of the family's circle of relatives, friends, and acquaintances had to be left out. In describing her school days, Laura limited her circle of schoolmates to Mary Power, Ida Brown, Minnie Johnson, Mamie Beardsley, and Nellie Oleson on the girls' side. Among the boys, there were Cap Garland, Ben Woodworth, Fred Gilbert, Arthur Johnson, and three others without last names given—Charley, Clarence, and Alfred. There were more storekeepers on Main Street than she mentions and more people in town whom she knew and interacted with, but to try to catalog them all would have been too confusing to her readers. Simplicity was one of her major goals. Therefore, Wilder resisted her daughter's suggestion to put more emphasis on kinfolk who passed through De Smet or temporarily resided there. As she explained in one letter to Rose, "I can't have any relatives cluttering up Hard Winter."[11] Although Wilder referred from time to time to people and episodes she had mentioned in previous books in the series, she resisted Lane's advice to highlight the activities of kinfolk as a means of charting their progress from book to book. While they were working on *The Long Winter*, Wilder groused "I truly don't see why Uncle Henry and Charley must be used in the rest of the books or be substituted for by some one who can. We have five principal characters who go all the way six counting Almanzo. That is enough to carry the story I know."[12]

Just as too many characters might clutter up the story, so could too many details. The plot had to *move*, which meant that Wilder had to select the episodes to be included carefully. In referring to the railroad camp at Silver Lake after the Ingalls family arrived there in the fall of 1879, for instance, Wilder wrote her daughter: "I didn't write a day by day narrative of those days in camp. I only wrote of the interesting events that happened and I thought were important."[13] Decisions about what to put in and what to leave out of stories are never easy to make, but Wilder chose to sacrifice historical detail in favor of narrative simplicity and movement. Thus, while she paid considerable attention to the store building that Pa constructed on the southeast corner of the intersection of Main Street and Second Street, she thought it would be unnecessary and probably confusing to readers to mention the building he had earlier constructed kitty-corner across the intersection, which Edward Couse bought to use as a hardware store. "It seemed to me not necessary to explain all this in the story. It would take too much space and I thought add nothing," she told Rose.[14]

Details were often modified to clarify or simplify the story or simply to enhance it. Although the true medical explanation of the disease that destroyed her sister Mary's eyesight remains elusive (Wilder variously described it to Lane as "some sort of spinal sickness," a "stroke," or "brain fever" resulting from the measles), in *By the*

Shores of Silver Lake Wilder says the cause was scarlet fever.[15] In another instance, Wilder admitted to her daughter that she had "stretched a point" in saying that she had gone with Pa to see the workers constructing the railroad, because in fact she had never actually seen the work going on. The story would have been diminished, however, had she merely related secondhand how the work was carried out.[16] And when she worked in town making shirts for Mr. Clayson (called Mr. Clancy in *Little Town on the Prairie*) and his mother-in-law, Mrs. White, she was not initially offered twenty-five cents a day plus dinner, as stated in the book, but rather got seventy-five cents a week without board, which was raised to a dollar and a half to induce her to stay on the job. Nevertheless, she quit after three weeks because her father objected to the nasty, violent atmosphere in the family. Although she mentions the familial conflicts in the book, her explanation there for her departure after six weeks was that the demand for shirts had dwindled after the spring rush ended.[17]

Minor changes of this sort were common in constructing the novels. The Bouchie school twelve miles south of town, for instance, becomes the Brewster school in the books;[18] the characters of Nellie Owens, Jennie Masters and Stella Gilbert were combined in that of Nellie Oleson;[19] and the construction of a new two-story grade school building in 1884 to accommodate the rapidly growing number of students was omitted from the narrative.[20] A more radical departure from fact can be observed in her decisions regarding the newly married couple that lived with her family in Pa's store building during the long winter of 1880-1881. The problem wasn't so much that Maggie Masters had a baby "much too soon after the time she was married," disgracing her parents, as that the couple's presence in the story would have drastically transformed the entire narrative. If they had been good, willing workers—which Wilder said they were not—it would have made survival for the family seem too easy and thus have eliminated their reliance on help from Almanzo, who hauled hay in from the country for them. It also would have undermined the book's whole premise about the hardships families suffered during the hard winter. On the other hand, to depict the couple as they actually were— lazy and unhelpful—would have been to "spoil the story." The only solution, in Wilder's view, was to eliminate them altogether, which she did.[21]

Although most of the modifications of historical fact were made by Wilder herself in drafting the novels, Lane also frequently modified, created, or elaborated upon scenes in order to flesh out the novel. One instance of this type of elaboration occurred in *By the Shores of Silver Lake* when Laura and Ma surprised Pa with a sackful of money they had earned by boarding settlers in their home before the first hotels went up in the new town of De Smet. Another example of it came at the end of the series in *These Happy Golden Years*. Wilder's description of her marriage to Almanzo in her draft manuscript required only 31 words: "It was eleven o'clock when they stood before Reverend Brown in the parsonage sitting room and were marrried with Ida and Elmer as witnesses and Mrs. Brown fluttering in the background." By the time Lane had finished her editorial work on it, the description of the wedding scene had been expanded into 254 words.[22]

Characters in the novels were introduced not because they necessarily had played especially important roles in the life of the family but because they could contribute in some way to the narrative line and help illustrate points that Wilder was trying to make. Reverend Alden, for example, had to be included because he was "directly responsible for Mary going to college." Charley, Louisa, and Uncle Henry were used to describe how people frequently stopped off for a time on their way west. Remarking on this point, Wilder told her daughter, "I think their appearing and disappearing as I have them do gives a feeling of the march westward, of the passing on of people and of their appearing unexpectedly. Also they make a contrast to the family left behind with clipped wings as Laura felt in that chapter."[23]

Just as characters were manipulated in telling the story,

events were molded, rearranged, or introduced to enhance dramatic impact. In *Little Town on the Prairie*, Lane added the episode where Laura first meets Almanzo Wilder when he picks her up as she walks out of Jake Hopp's newspaper office (where she had just obtained her new name cards) and offers her a ride to school in his buggy. Wilder's original draft of the book had Almanzo picking her up one noon as she was walking to school, but her original intention had been to have Laura and Almanzo meet when a blizzard closed the school toward the beginning of *The Long Winter*.[24] Somewhere along the line, she obviously changed her mind about how to introduce the relationship between the two; when they actually did meet is uncertain.

In drawing upon and rearranging the events of her own life in order to fictionalize them, Wilder, we can assume, worked with several rules in mind. She wanted to stick to the facts as much as possible and to the degree that she could call them up in her memory, but she would rearrange and modify those facts, where necessary, to fit the dramatic needs of narration. She would also simplify events and select those that would speed the story along and include characters and details that would make the points that she was trying to make about living on the prairie frontier.

In addition, however, Wilder was clearly in agreement with a rule that Lane repeatedly pounded home: She must make her descriptions vivid and memorable by imbuing them with color and emotion and life. Crucial to good writing, Lane believed, was the ability to *show* the reader what was happening rather than simply to *tell* what was going on. With experience, Wilder succeeded admirably at the task. "I don't see how anybody could improve on your use of words," Rose wrote her mother encouragingly in December 1937. "You are perfect in describing landscapes and things."[25] Wilder worked hard at getting just the right word, aiming not only for accuracy but also for tone and nuance. From time to time Lane noted lapses and demanded more description, as she did in the depiction of Mrs. McKee, a dressmaker in town who employed Laura for a while. In editing the draft of *These Happy Golden Years*, Lane noted on the manuscript, "Give us some description of Mrs. McKee, my goodness," and Wilder responded with: "She was tall and slender with kind blue eyes and a pleasant smile. Her light brown hair was worn in a knot at the back of her head."[26]

Lane's long experience at journalism, ghostwriting, and fiction writing gave her professional experience and a feel for the craft that her mother developed only over time and never to the degree that Lane had developed it. Although readers tended to assume that Wilder's vivid, evocative descriptions of people, places, and actions came naturallly to her, they actually came only with considerable assistance from Lane, emerging as a hard-won talent obtained through a great deal of practice and effort. Consider, for example, the simple, limp description of the train ride from Walnut Grove to Tracy, Minnesota, at the beginning of the family's trek to Dakota Territory as it was first put down in the "Pioneer Girl" manuscript of 1930:

> This was my first ride on a train, and was all too short, for leaving Walnut Grove in the morning we were at Tracy by noon, but short as it was I enjoyed it, while I helped Ma with Grace and the satchels and told Mary about everything I saw, for we were on our way again and going in the direction which always brought the happiest changes.[27]

In *By the Shores of Silver Lake*, written seven years later, Wilder took what she had said in that paragraph and lengthened it into a chapter. By then she had four published novels under her belt, and the draft of her fifth novel demonstrated a much surer command of narrative form.

> There was a clanking of car wheels, a "Puff! Puff!" from the engine and the train was moving.

The conductor came through the car toward them. He stopped at each seat and took the tickets. . . .

It was early morning and the wind blew in at the open window where Laura sat. She watched the last buildings of the town slip past. Then she could see away to the south across the Minnesota prairie. She had a glimpse of the grove of walnut trees that gave the name of Walnut Grove to the town.

After that grasslands and plowed fields and scattered farm buildings went hurrying past her window. Through the windows on the other side of the car she could see the long plume of black smoke, from the engine, drifting away on the wind.

It was grand to feel herself going so swiftly past houses and fields and she tried to tell Mary how quickly they were left behind.[28]

In the published version of the book, enhanced by Rose's polishing, the passage took on new lustre:

The train jerked, jolting her backward. Laura's chin bumped hard on the seat back, and her hat slid on her head. Again the train jerked, not so badly this time, and then it began to shiver and the depot moved.

"It's going!" Carrie cried out.

The shivering grew faster and louder, the depot slid backward, and under the car the wheels began to beat time. A rub-a-dubdub, a rub-a-dubdub, the wheels went, faster and faster. The lumberyard and the back of the church and the front of the schoolhouse went by, and that was the last of that town.

The whole car swayed now, in time to the clackety-clacking underneath it, and the black smoke blew by in melting rolls. A telegraph wire swooped up and down beyond the window. It did not really swoop, but it seemed to swoop because it sagged between the poles. It was fastened to green glass knobs that glittered in the sunshine and went dark when the smoke rolled above them. Beyond the wire, grasslands and fields and scattered farmhouses and barns went by.[29]

In some cases, Rose added material that fit with her increasingly conservative ideological stance during the 1930s. William Holtz's biography of her notes that the July Fourth episode in *Little Town on the Prairie* was expanded to include a speech that echoed Lane's commitment to freedom and to the kind of personal responsibility that goes along with it, a theme she paid particular attention to in her article ''Credo'' for the *Saturday Evening Post* in 1936.[30] However, additions and modifications of this sort were not numerous, nor did they change the plots materially, for Laura was in substantial agreement with her daughter ideologically and could easily have written something along similar lines.

Arranging the parts of the narrative in a logical, coherent whole proved a more difficult task than getting the parts themselves right. ''Your writing is really lovely,'' Rose told her mother while working on the manuscript of *By the Shores of Silver Lake*. ''It gets better and better. The only thing I would change at all is some of the structure. Learning how to handle material structurally is a hell of a job, I guess it's never done.'' Replying to her daughter's compliment, Wilder responded with a compliment of her own, ''I am glad you like my use of words and my descriptions, but without your fine touch, it would be a flop.''[31] The need for structure constituted a cardinal narrative rule for the mother-daughter team. Confident in her own understanding of structure, Rose continually preached its importance to her mother: ''You often write lines and whole paragraphs that I feel are what I would have written or anyway wish I had. What you haven't developed is structure, a kind of under-rhythm in the whole body of the writing, and a 'pointing up' here and there. And you often fail to put in detail.''[32]

The two argued long and hard, for example, about the beginning of *By the Shores of Silver Lake*, Wilder wanting it to start at the railroad depot with Ma and the girls ready to depart for Dakota Territory, Lane pressing for an initial chapter or two that would describe the hard times in Minnesota that forced the family to leave. Wilder eventually came around to Lane's position on the matter. At one point, she told her in frustration: "Change the beginning of the story if you want. Do anything you please with the damn stuff if you will fix it up."[33] Likewise, mother and daughter achieved a meeting of the minds on how to start *The Long Winter*, Wilder originally deferring to Rose's suggestion that it begin with the strangeness of geese not stopping at the lake on their way south and later beginning with Laura helping her father with haying in the fall.[34] While she was working on that book, Wilder expected to finish the series with one more volume, to be entitled *Prairie Girl*, but eventually this material emerged as two separate books, *Little Town on the Prairie* and *These Happy Golden Years*, which completed the series of children's books. The posthumous publication of *The First Four Years*, which was aimed at an adult audience, carried the story into Wilder's first years of marriage.

Each of these books expressed clearly defined themes and were constructed around narrative structures adequate for explicating them, although in the process of composition Wilder sometimes despaired of being able to find a central thread on which to hang her narrative. *By the Shores of Silver Lake* begins with the family's plans to depart Plum Creek and establish a homestead further west in Dakota Territory; it ends with the family moving into their new claim shanty on a 160-acre plot one mile southeast of De Smet. Although deferring to her daughter's judgment on how the book should begin, Wilder clearly envisioned its central theme—homesteading. "The idea of the homestead is never lost sight of," she wrote. "All the other things, R.R. building riots, winter in the surveyors house, living in town awhile are obstacles to be overcome before the family would have a home again. . . . The book is bound to be mostly about the R.R. and town, for securing the homestead *in spite of difficul-*

ties is the story and being at home on the homestead at last is the climax and finish."[35]

Establishing a central theme for her next volume, *The Long Winter*, presented a harder task. "I can't seem to find a plot, or pattern as you call it," she wrote Lane in exasperation. "There seems to be nothing to it only the struggle to live, through the winter, until spring comes again. This of course they all did. But is it strong enough, or can it be made strong enough to supply the necessary thread running all through the book?"[36] Ultimately, however, the book turned into one of the most memorable volumes in the series, because the elemental struggle between the town's residents and the forces of nature set the stage for so much drama and heroism. Failure in this contest would have meant not merely defeat or disappointment, but death. The book begins around August 1880 with the observation of peculiar signs pointing to a hard winter. It ends nine months later with the celebration of Christmas in May, with the hard winter over and the trains running again. In the meantime, Laura, her family, and their neighbors have faced up to and triumphed over a series of challenges, large and small—walking into a strange town, getting lost in the slough on the way home, entering school, running low on food, running out of coal and kerosene, and people going stir-crazy because of the dearth of human contact.

In *Little Town on the Prairie* and *These Happy Golden Years*, as in all of her books, Wilder followed the narrative rule of establishing a central theme and then organizing her plot around a series of challenges or conflicts to be confronted and resolved. After the challenges of homesteading in *By the Shores of Silver Lake* and grappling with the weather in *The Long Winter*, the problem presented in *Little Town on the Prairie* is that of negotiating adolescence—learning how to relate to other people in school and in the town. The book starts with Laura getting a job in town so she can earn money to help send Mary to college, and it ends with her leaving town for her first teaching job in the country. Meanwhile, her attitude toward town living has changed, as she has come to appreciate the activities and relationships available there. Challenges and conflicts in this book include working in town, earning money for Mary's college education, being uncomfortable among strangers, shooing blackbirds out of the corn patch, attending school, being ganged up on by her teacher—Miss Wilder—and Nellie Oleson, performing in the school exhibition, and finally obtaining her teaching certificate and going out to the Brewster school.

These Happy Golden Years chronicled Laura's later adolescence and maturation as she goes from being a schoolgirl and schoolteacher to marrying Almanzo Wilder. The book begins with her moving south of town to the Brewster school to teach, and it ends with her and Almanzo moving to their new home north of town. Meanwhile, Laura has successfully gotten through her first school term as a teacher, survived several life-threatening sleigh rides through the cold, written her first school composition (on ambition), been courted by Almanzo, and decided to marry him. By now she has begun to take challenges in her stride that had seemed threatening or fearsome just a few years earlier. Laura has been transformed from a schoolgirl into a young woman.

One final rule that Wilder followed, and one that Lane insisted upon, related to point of view. Except for *The First Four Years*, which Wilder never submitted for publication, the novels were all classified as children's books, and they were written with children in mind. The point of view was basically Wilder's at the age she would have been at the time the action was taking place, although Wilder could not maintain that pose with perfect consistency. Information that Laura could not have observed or known about was introduced in various ways. Generally the books were written from a limited omniscient point of view, in which the narration describes events primarily as they were seen through Laura's eyes but in which the reader also learns about some things that Laura could not possibly have directly observed.[37] ''You MUST keep in mind to write the whole thing from Laura's point of view," Lane reminded her mother. "Arrange the material so that she can actually see, hear, experience as much as possible."[38] When Lane worried that some material might sound too adult, her mother defended her approach by reminding Lane that Laura, after all, was growing older and more mature and that several factors made her seem more grown-up than children the same age during the 1930s. "I don't see how we can spare what you call adult stuff, for that makes the story," she wrote Lane. "It was there and Laura knew and understood it."[39]

The writing of the novels was a learning process, and the collaboration between mother and daughter, while sometimes strained, was generally successful. What had caused problems in the beginning frequently was totally forgotten as time went on. Each book was worked out in outline before the writing began but was modified in the process of conceptualization and actual composition. Only in the process of rewriting did the final result take shape. As Wilder described it to Lane, "The only way I can write is to wander along with the story, then rewrite and rearrange and change it everywhere."[40] If that can be considered the last rule of narration—rewrite and rewrite again—it certainly was not the least. The rules followed by the mother-daughter team served them well, and the *Little Town* series took its place among the classics of American children's literature.

7 / Textbook History versus Lived History

Whatever else they might be—stories, myths, memory, autobiography—the Little Town novels are also history. Although Wilder did not consciously set out to write history, she gradually realized that in writing the novels she was re-creating a moment in the historical past. She alluded to this point in her Detroit Book Week speech in October 1937, recalling the response to the publication of her first book, *Little House in the Big Woods*, five years earlier:

> When to my surprise the book made such a success and children from all over the U.S. wrote to me begging for more stories, I began to think what a wonderful childhood I had had. How I had seen the whole frontier, the woods, the Indian country of the great plains, the frontier towns, the building of railroads in wild, unsettled country, homesteading and farmers coming in to take possession. I realized that I had seen and lived it all—all the successive phases of the frontier, first the frontiersman, then the pioneer, then the farmers and the towns. Then I understood that in my own life I represented a whole period of American history.[1]

"I wanted the children now to understand more about the beginning of things," Wilder told her Detroit audience, "to know what is behind the things they see—what it is that made America as they know it."[2] Children loved

the books, and their teachers did, too. The Little Town
novels made studying history fun; it hardly seemed like
history at all, at least as they had known it. A teacher
from Chesterton, Indiana, wrote to tell Wilder that she
was using *Little House in the Big Woods* in her social
studies class as a textbook for learning about pioneer life.
"The incidents related are told in such a charming manner that my pupils greeted each reading with a round of
applause," she enthusiastically reported. "Your books
help us in our history work more than the other history
books because they showed us how the settlers came to
the prairie," a student in Los Angeles wrote. The stories
made history come alive. A sixth-grade class in La Crosse,
Wisconsin, wrote to say that the stories made them feel
like pioneers on the prairie. "Some of us who didn't like
History before now like it a great deal," they noted. "Every day we wait for story time to see what happened
next."[3]

Although youngsters were roundly enthusiastic about
the stories Wilder recounted in the novels, some students
wondered how she was able to remember so vividly events
that had happened five or six decades earlier. "How can
you remember all of the things you did when you were a
little girl?" the student from Los Angeles inquired. Another young reader wondered: "How can you remember
all you wrote in your books? How can you remember everything since you were a little girl?"[4] These fans might
have been startled to discover how their heroine's method
of studying history as a schoolgirl had helped her culti-
vate her memory and thus aided her in recalling things
that had happened long before.

Rote memory was the principal tool for learning when
Laura was going to school. History textbooks encouraged
this approach by highlighting important names, dates,
and facts and by including special sections at the front or
back of the book filled with time lines and lists of historical events and dates to be memorized.[5] As a young girl,
Laura took pride in her scholarship, and if a story she related in *Little Town on the Prairie* accurately reflects

what went on in her history classes, they resembled nineteenth-century classrooms everywhere in emphasizing the systematic memorization of long lists of historical events in sequential order. At a school exhibition in December 1882, when Laura was fifteen years old, she warmed up with the other students by ''reciting geography,'' diagramming sentences on the blackboard, and doing mental arithmetic. ''It would be shameful,'' she thought, ''to fail to answer, or to make a mistake, before all those people and Pa and Ma, but she was not frightened.'' During these preliminary exercises, which elicited great applause from the audience, Laura silently kept going over and over in her mind the chronological sequences she would soon have to recite, dreading the possibility of failure.[6]

Her part in the program, in conjunction with her friend Ida Brown, was ''to recite the whole of American history, from memory.'' Ida was to recite the second half, Laura the first half.[7] When her time arrived, she began: ''America was discovered by Christopher Columbus in 1492. Christopher Columbus, a native of Genoa in Italy, had long sought permission to make a voyage toward the west in order to discover a new route to India. At that time Spain was ruled by the united crowns of . . .'' On and on she proceeded, through the Spanish and French explorers, the lost colony at Roanoke, the Jamestown and Massachusetts Bay settlements, and the purchase of Manhattan by the Dutch. Soon she was really warmed up. ''She told of the new vision of freedom and equality in the New World, she told of the old oppressions of Europe and of the war against tyranny and despotism, of the war for independence of the thirteen new States, and of how the Constitution was written and these thirteen States united.'' Continuing through the presidencies of Washington, Adams, Jefferson, Madison, and Monroe, she followed the course of American history until, west from the Missouri, traders ventured down the Santa Fe Trail to Mexico and wagons loaded with settlers rolled into Kansas. Her ordeal over, Laura sat down to a roar of applause that continued until Mr. Owen, the teacher, stopped it. Ida Brown, in carrying the story from the administration of John Quincy Adams through that of Rutherford B. Hayes, "did not make one mistake."[8]

Much can be inferred from this episode about the history instruction of the time. It was nationalistic, patriotic, and didactic. The past pointed to the present and reached toward the future, explaining the high degree of progress and perfection that the nation had achieved. It was also conventional and elitist. Politics, as highlighted by presidential administrations, provided a framework for pigeonholing historical facts and focusing students' attention. Presidents, generals, explorers, and other great leaders acted as the crucial determinants of history, while pioneers, workers, and farmers played out the minor roles that were assigned to them, receiving little attention. History was sequential; it moved. Understanding history required putting facts into chronological order and observing how one development necessarily led to another. To know history, therefore, was to know what these facts were; to demonstrate one's knowledge, a person recited them. Thus, if one could memorize everything and avoid any mistakes, one would "know history."

The central, and usually only, pedagogical tool for learning (that is, memorizing) this type of history was the textbook. Since there were few well-qualified teachers on the frontier, reliance on the textbook was not entirely a bad thing.[9] Studies that have been done of history textbooks used during the post–Civil War period note that they leaned toward a didactic, sequential, fact-based, moralistic, teleological approach. Along with other subjects in the curriculum, history was supposed to be more than an intellectual exercise; it had important lessons to teach. "Little children," admonished the author of a selection in a reader published in 1882, "you must seek rather to be good than wise."[10] History, for its part, could engender patriotism; teach the virtues of hard work, persistence, honesty, and sobriety; and offer role models to help build character in young people.[11]

The textbook that Laura studied for her school exhibition performance was Edward Taylor's *A Brief Account of
the American People for Schools*, published in 1878 by
George Sherwood and Company of Chicago. She later presented her copy of the book to the Detroit Public Library
along with the manuscripts of two of her novels. On the
inside cover, in her schoolgirl handwriting, she had penciled, "Laura Ingalls, 1882." At the beginning of the book,
right after the table of contents, were time charts listing
dates of important events from 1700 to 1877, which could
be used to summarize and emphasize key episodes and
dates for recitation. In the preface to the book, Taylor explained the utility of the Chart of Events:

> To most minds the mastery of dates is drudgery,
> and in the average school few exercises are more bar-
> ren and profitless. No claim of originality in the gen-
> eral plan of the Chart is made. A. S. Lyman, in his
> Chart of Universal History, used it thirty years ago. It
> has been found that the association of an event with
> its relative place in the stream of time remains im-
> pressed on the mind long after the arbitrary memory
> of a date has passed away. It is a method approved by
> experience, and not a scheme dictated by fancy.[12]

The author went on to explain that he had devoted more
than the usual attention to political contests, educational
affairs, industrial development, public opinion, domestic
manners, and, in general, "the development of our national life."

Unlike other textbooks, which relegated as much as 45
percent of their space to military and battle history, Taylor's did not "make a specialty of military details. It is not
'a drum and trumpet history.'"[13] The book highlighted
important facts by using boldface type and provided review sections to assist the student in memorization. With
events summarized in short phrases or slogans, the student could more readily separate the significant from the

unimportant. In the section on John Adams, for instance, topics highlighted in boldface type included:

trouble with France
three special envoys
hostilities began
war was averted
death of Washington
death of Patrick Henry
the Second Census
the Westward Movement
Social and Domestic Life
public conveyance
party spirit
presidential campaign
the result
electoral college

Within a basically chronological framework, using presidential administrations to organize the material, the author did more than simply describe national development. He celebrated it. "The paramount idea," he advised his readers, "has been to show the learner the steps of progress by which we have become a great nation." In order to achieve his didactic purposes, he presented the facts in the way he believed most conducive to understanding and retention, following accepted pedagogical principles: "The narrative, it is thought, will be found to be full of facts and those *the essential ones*."[14]

Such an approach functioned to develop character and to reinforce accepted values, and if we accept Wilder's description of her own performance, it also worked effectively to fix basic factual knowledge in students' memories. But this kind of history provided little information about the lives of ordinary people and how they changed over time. When Wilder began writing her autobiographical reminiscences in 1930, the world of her childhood seemed distant and blurred. The post–Civil War western frontier had already entered into folklore, described and celebrated in the popular culture through radio programs, movies, comic books, novels, and magazines. The adventures of the cattle frontier, with its shootouts and cowboys and Indians, had driven itself deeply into the public consciousness while the more mundane development of the agricultural frontier remained vaguer in people's minds.

Children were eager to read Wilder's stories about that more homely frontier—the westward movement of farmers and townspeople as they moved into Dakota Territory. By the time she was writing, the locus of historical authority for her had shifted from textbook authors to her own memory, and the lives of ordinary people, not just those of statesmen and generals or other exceptional people, had been invested with historical significance. Perhaps not coincidentally, professional historians were by this time beginning to acknowledge the validity of other, nontraditional forms of history. During the early 1900s, Progressive historians had emphasized the need for studying social history and for including ordinary people in their accounts.[15] During the twenties and thirties, historians like Charles Beard and Carl Becker intensified the demand for a more varied approach to the past by arguing for diverse perspectives and supporting the validity of personal interpretations. In 1932, at about the same time that Wilder began writing her novels, Becker, in "Everyman His Own Historian," sounded a clarion call for a new kind of everyday history that could be distilled from unrelated sources, including newspapers, books, movies, radio, and gossip.[16]

The frontier that Wilder described in her novels had already been firmly established among the dominant group of American historians as the primary factor in explaining American historical development. Frederick Jackson Turner had emphasized the forces of nationalism, democracy, individualism, and innovation in his frontier thesis.[17] For Turnerians, the frontier was history; for Laura Ingalls Wilder, it was memory. Yet, as she noted in her

Detroit Book Week speech, her purpose in telling her stories was to write another kind of history.

Wilder emphasized that she did not invent her stories: they were *true*, they were *factual*. In corresponding with Lane about *By the Shores of Silver Lake*, for instance, she tried to explain how girls' behavior in her own day had been more demure, reserved, and innocent than it had become by the 1930s. "This is a true story," Wilder said of her description of life in the 1880s, "and supposes they had a different (almost) civilization."[18] In later years, Lane vehemently defended the factual accuracy of her mother's books. She demanded that William Anderson modify a statement in *The Story of the Ingalls* in which he said that the Ingalls family had had several neighbors in the vicinity during their first winter in Dakota Territory. This statement implied, Lane fumed, that her mother was a liar. "You will please correct your proposed publication to accord with my mother's statement in her books," she wrote Anderson. "I cannot permit publication of a slander of my mother's character, and I shall not do so."[19] To Lane, the question of factual accuracy was crucial; the books' value and her mother's reputation depended on it. "My mother's repeated and emphatic claim that her books are 'true' stories, plus the fact that records exist to verify that claim . . . give her a strong motive for accuracy," she told Anderson. "Mr. Sherwood and Mr. Boast, merely repeating hear-say, . . . no doubt believe their statements to be true, but have nothing to lose if they are mistaken about a date; why should they *work* for accuracy? If my mother's books are not absolutely accurate, she will be dis-credited as a person and as a writer."[20]

Indeed, Wilder and Lane both went to considerable lengths to ensure factual accuracy in their writings, and both worried that others might find a mistake. They communicated through letters and in the margins of manuscripts as the novels went through the editing process. They worried about the tiniest of details, taking great pains to make sure that they had geographical locations properly fixed, time sequences correctly dated, people correctly identified, words accurately spelled. In gauging the distance between De Smet and Brookings for *The Long Winter*, for instance, Wilder indicated to Lane how she had made her estimate and said that she would write to someone in De Smet to verify it. "It won't do to have it wrong," she remarked.[21] When the editors at Harper's took the liberty of modifying some spellings (e.g., changing "plow" to "plough," in the English fashion) in *On the Banks of Plum Creek* without informing Wilder or Lane, the latter was infuriated. Had she realized what they were doing, she wrote her mother, she would have "raised hell." Hoping to avoid another such occurrence, she instructed, "Do not EVER let these damn ignoramuses in publishing offices DARE to correct your copy. I can not look at PLUM CREEK without getting so mad I am sick."[22]

When the *Saturday Evening Post* published her eight-part serial "Free Land" in early 1938, Lane grew almost apoplectic when she learned from Wilder that grain threshing normally did not take place as early in the summer as she had described it, but rather continued late into the fall and winter. "I am completely wrecked by threshing being in cold weather," she wrote her mother. "I have made a frightful fool of myself in SEP and book, and ten thousand readers will write in to say so, and it is too late now to re-write the damn thing. . . . Well, there's nothing to do but grit the teeth and bear it. 'Dear Gentle Reader (and editors of the SEP), You are quite right. Threshing was in October, and I know nothing whatever about what I'm writing about, yours sincerely, and thanking you for your kind correction, RWL.' Ten thousand of 'em."[23]

Lane worked hard while writing *Let the Hurricane Roar* and *Free Land* to get her facts right, picking the brains of both her parents for details of life on the frontier. Wilder, in contrast, had the advantage of writing about her own experiences, but she had to recall events that had occurred fifty years earlier. To supplement and stimulate her memory, she began in 1925 to write to her aunt Martha Carpenter to get some old recipes and other information to use

De Smet *News* office on an Old Settlers' Day in the late 1940s. There are Harvey Dunn paintings on the wall and two Wilder novels on the counter. *(Courtesy South Dakota State Historical Society)*

for an article in the *Ladies Home Journal* about her grandmother's cooking.[24] Later, while working on the novels, she and Almanzo drove back to De Smet three times—in 1931, 1938, and 1939—to visit their old haunts. She also dug out old mementoes and other scraps of evidence that she had saved to assist her in bringing the old days back to mind, and she drew a map of the town to help remind herself of what it had been like while she was growing up there.[25]

Book reviewers and admiring readers praised her exceptional ability to incorporate telling details into her stories. Yet she admitted to Lane how frustrating the process of trying to dredge up old memories could be. In 1937, several years after she had begun writing about her Dakota Territory experiences, she discovered that the whole period had taken on a dull appearance in her mind. People, places, and events no longer stood out as vividly in her memory as they had just several years earlier when she began writing her recollections. Somehow she had to force those memories to the surface. The following year, while working on *The Long Winter*, she complained, "Strange how my memory fails me on all but the high lights."[26]

Rather than remaining constant, Wilder's powers of recall seem to have gone through cycles and to have been affected by varying moods and stimuli. A name from her past once elicited nothing in her mind when it was first mentioned, but that evening, just as she began to fall asleep, Wilder conjured up the old schoolhouse that she had attended in Burr Oak, Iowa, and could visualize the woodshed snuggled alongside it with its slanted roof that the children used to step out onto when their teachers were absent from the room.[27]

Sometimes Laura was astonished by how much she had tucked into the deep recesses of her mind beyond her consciousness. In preparing to write the books set around De Smet, she queried her sister Grace about the wildflowers that had carpeted the prairie when the family arrived there. Grace's inventory—which included wild onions, purple and yellow violets, sheep sorrel, yellow buttercups, tiger lilies, and wild geraniums—brought everything back to her. "To think that I could have forgotten all this which comes back to me now," Wilder wrote Lane. "That's why the sooner I write my stuff the better."[28]

Just how reliable was Wilder's memory? That question continues to intrigue scholars and readers alike. Recent studies of how memory functions deny that it simply and faithfully reproduces past events and experiences and then stores them someplace in the brain. Instead, memory is selective and creative, serving the needs of the present. It is constructed, not simply reproduced. In the construction process, people actively and creatively distort, omit, combine, and reorganize past events as they establish their own interpretations of what happened. In the words of Edmund Blair Bolles, "Emotions, perceptions, and reminders all stir the imagination, and imagination, not storage, is the basis of memory."[29]

Pierre Nora observes that memory "remains in permanent evolution, open to the dialectic of remembering and forgetting, unconscious of its successive deformations, vulnerable to manipulation and appropriation, susceptible to being long dormant and periodically revived. History, on the other hand, is the reconstruction, always problematic and incomplete, of what is no longer."[30] Parallel processes occur in memory, which is individual, and history, which is collective. In either case, there exists a tendency to fix a definition of the past in concrete terms that are more definite and certain than the evidence justifies. The term for this process is *reification*. What, at first consideration, might seem vague, shapeless, and indefinite can, upon further reflection and inquiry, become solidified in one's thinking, either as memory or as history. In the case of history, the formulation is open to challenge from contrary evidence, logic, argumentation, or testimony. In the case of individual memory, making a distinction between the real and the imaginary—between "what really happened" and what we may only be conjuring up in our mind—is more difficult.

In either instance, the process takes place within a social context, meaning that a variety of pressures impinge on how memories take form and how history gets written. What got written in the history textbooks used by Laura was influenced by the reigning climate of opinion, the political context, institutional requirements, and professional practices. What Wilder remembered of her childhood and what she chose to write about likewise reflected her values, aspirations, social environment, and climate of opinion. Her books could not give a complete and fully accurate account of the frontier or even of her own experiences; rather, they presented a selective one, as must be the case with all such interpretations.

Since she was writing for a juvenile audience, she could not write about subjects that were not fit for children to know about, even if, as a child herself, she had been aware of them. Matters that might embarrass her family were also out-of-bounds.[31] Wilder sometimes constructed composite characters and rearranged chronology in order to simplify her narrative line and to retain the interest of her readers. Always she endeavored to present her stories from the point of view of a girl who was the age Laura had been at the time the action occurred. The result was to eliminate almost completely social conflicts and political controversies, which children would not have understood or been aware of. This was history with a difference—a kind of social history that excluded social classes, social conflict, and most social problems. To be sure, the problems involved with drinking and the temperance movement were not excluded, relations between Indians and whites provided an instance of ethnic conflict, and family violence was alluded to. But to a considerable degree hers was sanitized history that excluded unpleasant realities.

No wonder her work appealed to so many readers. Both children and adults could be attracted to the vivid portrayal of characters, the concrete description of details, and the delightful stories of school suppers, Fourth of July celebrations, and railroad construction. The stories she told were meant not only to describe but to impart valuable lessons. They frequently contained a moral, which was often made explicit. Writing for children, Wilder was on firm ground. But when she tried her hand at an adult novel with grown-up themes—the story of economic hardship and personal heartbreak during the first four years of Laura and Almanzo's marriage—she found herself on much more difficult terrain and never submitted the manuscript for publication.

Like Wilder's novels of the frontier, the history textbooks she and her schoolmates read provided selective versions of the past. They, too, were meant not only to describe the past but also to guide behavior, inculcate virtue, and undergird morale. Both presented their own heroes and heroines: in the textbooks they were Washington, Jefferson, Jackson, and the rest; in the novels Ma, Pa, and the others. Both omitted certain things: the novels avoided themes unfit for children; the textbooks things unconducive to patriotic sentiment. Both used narrative to provide structure and meaning for the events they strung together. One used memory to convey values and ideals dear to their author; the other used history to do the same for the broader general public.

In this fashion, the Little Town novels, so different in form from the history books that Laura Ingalls had studied as a child, functioned in similar ways to achieve comparable results. Memory and history were important in the novels not so much for the past they recalled as for the present they invoked. They enabled individuals to function more efficiently within the community, and they supported communities in their need to preserve social cohesion and morale. In that sense, they were valuable. But for people who valued accuracy, critical analysis, honest difference, and the inclusion of groups and values that had been left out, new kinds of stories and history would have to be written.

Just as her mother did, Lane wrote her stories of the Dakota frontier not only to entertain but to edify. History, she firmly believed, had lessons to impart. When *Let the Hurricane Roar* came out serially in the *Saturday Evening Post* at the nadir of the Depression in late 1932, she gratefully copied in her journal a long letter from Carl Wisner describing *Hurricane* as "the kind of story which the American reading public needs to get back in thought to the American philosophy of life, in a time of great stress and personal perplexity for us all." Rose no doubt agreed with his criticism of the pessimistic brand of realism that, in his view, distorted the past. He preferred to focus on "the fine theme of achievement and artistic sense of mastery of a job and creation of something 'out of the raw.' " The value of history depended on factual accuracy, but it also required balanced perspective: "If the American philosophy of life is to be understood and correctly interpreted, the pioneer experiences must be given realistically, but with the optimistic faith of the pioneers. Failure to do this has given us the 'Main Streets' without any understanding of the background."[32]

Wilder's first novel had been published that year, and

Lane was in the process of editing her second one, *Farmer Boy*, which came out the following year. Meanwhile, during early 1933 Rose formulated a grandiose plan of her own for an "American novel in many volumes, an enormous canvas, covering horizontally a continent, vertically all classes." It would focus on relationships and conflicts among groups and classes and show how power defined these interactions. Thus, it would concentrate on the very types of themes and questions that her mother, for the most part, so studiously avoided. Making a preliminary inventory of the groups she wanted to portray, she listed workers, radicals, clerks, bankers, petite bourgeoisie, big businessmen, intellectuals, scientists, and politicians. "American history, therefore our life now, is a swirl of currents across this landscape. Cultural currents deflected, altered, by economic (based on geographic?) and geographic conditions." The task would require ten novels, she estimated, and their plots would combine into "one large canvas, mosaic, expressing great ideas, great and true emotions, and being a picture of American life today. The contemporary scene. Conflicting forces must be seen clearly. The past from which they come must be felt—and the future. Life and death and love and hate—the human heart."[33]

Lane never completed or ever even really got started on this huge historical assignment.[34] Instead she worked during the 1930s on a history of Missouri (never published), another novel about the Dakota frontier, and many smaller writing assignments that kept the money flowing in. The energies that might have gone into her own project were partly absorbed by the task of editing her mother's novels, which ironically emerged as a multivolume history similar to what Lane had contemplated writing herself.[35] But where the daughter had conceived of a broad canvas ranging far and wide across the landscape and tracing historical causes back to their European sources, the mother limited her story geographically and temporally to the midwestern frontier where she herself had grown up. Where daughter thought abstractly in big ideas, mother stuck to the concrete and to her own experience. Where daughter relied on research, mother depended mostly on memory. Where daughter wanted to concentrate on social conflict, progress, and power relationships, mother simply wanted to tell stories that she had heard or to describe what she had witnessed. Both drew lessons from the stories they had to tell, but those of the daughter were processed through her own wide reading of history and consideration of scholarly and polemical studies while those of the mother were filtered through her own personal experience.

Thus, it is ironic that Lane, who had aspired to write history in the form of a grand historical novel, ultimately failed at it while her mother, who had simply desired to preserve in memory some of the stories she had heard as a child, made a valuable contribution to history. As soon as they were published, Wilder's novels were recognized as such by readers, reviewers, students, and teachers,[36] and they eventually established themselves as a classic statement about frontier history. Maria Cimino called the novels "a lasting record of a significant phase in American social history." George McGovern observed that through her novels Wilder "rewove her life into history."[37]

But though they are a form of history, the novels also transformed their materials into myth, for they created a selective, nostalgic, elegiac view of the past. They occupy what C. Vann Woodward calls "the twilight zone that lies between living memory and written history," which "is one of the favorite breeding places of mythology."[38] And, as all good myths do, they reflect the values, goals, and purposes of their author and of the readers they were aimed at. For this we can be grateful, because they thereby provide keys for unlocking a popular mindset of the 1930s and 1940s as well as the lived history of a significant late-nineteenth-century agricultural frontier.

8 / De Smet as Frontier Destination and Way Station

Part of the appeal of Wilder's children's novels is that they embody one of the central features of the American experience—the westward movement. For early-twentieth-century devotees of Frederick Jackson Turner and his frontier thesis of American development, the westward-moving frontier is *the* definitive element of the American story and explains, better than anything else, the peculiar character of our institutions, social relations, and national character.[1] As just one family in a vast stream of westward migrants, the Ingallses epitomized the hopes and the fears, the dreams and the harsh realities that accompanied this mighty rush as the family lived in Wisconsin, Kansas, Minnesota, Iowa, and finally, Dakota Territory.

Their prolonged wanderings remind us that for many families the journey was not a simple unidirectional movement westward toward the setting sun. On the contrary, it was frequently necessary for families to backtrack and retrace their steps as economic prospects brightened or faded or as weather conditions, natural disasters, Indian uprisings, and other factors influenced their decisions. The Ingalls family's peripatetic wandering fit more closely George W. Pierson's model of the "moving American," who bounced around to and fro in no particular direction, than it did Frederick Jackson Turner's paradigm of the constantly westward-moving frontiersman. Echoing the observations of numerous commentators since Tocqueville, Pierson insisted upon the central importance of the "M Factor"—movement, migration, and mobility—in American history, pointing out that migrants often zigged and zagged, advanced and retreated, in unpredictable fashion rather than tracing a constant pattern to the West as suggested by the Turner Thesis.[2] Charles and Caroline Ingalls and their four girls were caught up in this churning process, which was common on the frontier and continues to characterize American movers, who remain the most mobile people in the world.[3]

In a letter to Lane written in early 1938, while they were thrashing out the manuscript for *The Long Winter*, Wilder described pioneer mobility: "I used Charley, Louisa and Uncle Henry to show how people made stops on the way to the far west. How families parted were again united and parted again, casually, without any heroics as people now say—'Well! I'll be seein ya.' . . . I think their appearing and disappearing as I have them do gives a feeling of the march westward, of the passing on of people and of their appearing unexpectedly."[4] The Ingalls family conformed to a common stereotype of the frontier family—a husband constantly lured westward into the unknown and the reluctant wife who resisted moving and who wished to stay put and enjoy the benefits of settled life.[5]

For some of the people Wilder wrote about, De Smet was the final destination. Ma and Pa remained in De Smet—Pa died there in 1902 in the house he had built on Third Street, and Ma lingered on until 1924. Mary also died there in 1928. They were all buried in the cemetery south of town, and later, Grace, who had married Nate Dow and moved to Manchester, eight miles west of De Smet, and Carrie, who had married David Swanzey and moved to Keystone in the Black Hills, were buried alongside them.[6]

Only Laura's grave is missing. Although her parents and sisters all stayed in South Dakota, she is buried in Mansfield, Missouri, where she moved with her husband Almanzo in 1894. It was she, in the end, who continued the family's peripatetic ways with one final leap to the "land of the big red apple" in the Missouri Ozarks.[7] There she lived the remaining sixty-three years of her life, there she wrote the books about her childhood, and there she accepted the accolades that came to her for having captured in print the adventure and drama of the frontier experience.

Laura and Almanzo's departure from De Smet in 1894 reminds us that for many of the town's inhabitants and surrounding rural dwellers, the "little town on the prairie" was not the final destination. As we read the stories we think about where the characters came from—the Ingallses from Wisconsin, the Wilders from New York, the Olesons from Minnesota, and so on. Although we may wonder what happened to them later, the books do not tell us. For some, De Smet was only a way station. Big Jerry, Uncle Hi, and Aunt Docia, and others involved in the building of the railroad moved on; Brother Alden and his assistant likewise stayed on the move; Mr. Edwards returned from time to time to let his friends know his whereabouts. For the most part, however, our attention is directed backward in time—toward where the people in the story came *from* rather than where they were headed *to*.

This way of viewing Wilder's novels converges with the way we usually look at migration patterns. We tend to focus on sources rather than on destinations, partly because surviving records make it easier to discover starting points than destinations—it is generally easier to investigate the background of people once they have located in a particular place than it is to try to trace where they went later. We usually trace people's origins back to the states in the East, and ultimately to Europe, and seldom ask where they wound up in the end.[8]

Although the executives of the Chicago and North Western Railroad in Chicago never gave the matter a thought, their extension of a line through eastern Dakota Territory during a census year was fortuitous for later historians interested in the character of the population that first came to the area. When the census taker, John H. Carroll, made his rounds through Kingsbury County in

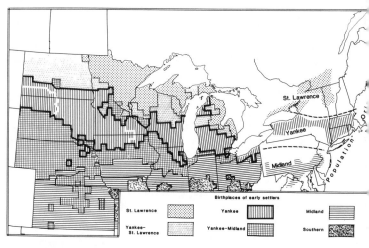

Yankeeland in the Middle West. *(Source:* Journal of Geography *85 (1986): 196; reprinted with permission)*

the summer of 1880, he recorded the origins, ages, and occupations of everyone residing in the area. Beginning on June 7, 1880, he counted 116 residents in the brand-new town of De Smet (the only town in the county according to the census). He then proceeded through the rest of Kingsbury County from west to east until June 25, when C. C. Ramsey took over and finished up the last several townships.[9]

The thirty-one-year-old Carroll, who listed himself, his twenty-five-year-old wife, Sara, and their infant son Louis at the top of the first census sheet, typified the settlers who started businesses in the brand-new towns established during the great Dakota boom of the early 1880s. A Pennsylvanian by birth, he was the son of English parents. Sara had been born in Michigan, her father in Vermont, and her mother in New York. Before coming to Dakota Territory in 1880, the young family had lived in Minnesota, where Louis was born. With regard to their places of birth, the Carrolls were typical of the stream of people who spread out across the northern tier of states during ''the Yankee migration'' of the nineteenth century. John C. Hudson gave the name Yankeeland to the areas dominated by this migratory group—northern Ohio, southern

Michigan, northeastern Illinois, southeastern Wisconsin, southwestern Minnesota, and much of the Dakotas. This stream of migration derived primarily from the Yankee cultural hearth, which Hudson identified as the states of Massachusetts, Connecticut, and Rhode Island and the central and southern parts of New York and northern Pennsylvania. (A cultural hearth is a region with a more or less unified culture whose characteristics get diffused when its inhabitants begin to migrate into new areas).[10] People like the Carrolls carried with them considerable cultural baggage—including the Protestant religion, Republican politics, devotion to family, strong work habits, chicken pie suppers, and lyceum groups—that perpetuated the values and lifestyles of New England and New York throughout this section of the upper Midwest.[11]

The Carrolls, like Laura and Almanzo Wilder, did not remain permanently in De Smet. Carroll, who listed himself as clerk of the district court in the 1880 census, took up banking and real estate (his office, north across Second Street from Pa's store building, is mentioned in *The Long Winter*) and later entered politics, serving as the town's first mayor and rising to become Speaker of the House in the state legislature. During the teens he and his wife moved to St. Petersburg, Florida, where he profited from the burgeoning real estate boom there. "We are having great times down here," the inveterate speculator wrote the editor of the De Smet *News* in 1923, "large numbers of tourists, more automobiles than blackbirds, and things booming."[12]

Analysis of the 1880 census data reveals that the residents of De Smet clearly represented John Hudson's "Yankeeland" dwellers. Wisconsin and New York ranked first and second as places of birth for the newly arrived townspeople, with Ohio, Michigan, and Illinois just behind them. Pennsylvania also ranked high and would continue to export large numbers of its people to join John H. Carroll in De Smet and the surrounding rural countryside. Although Hudson places Pennsylvania in another "cultural hearth," which he calls the Midland, he contends the

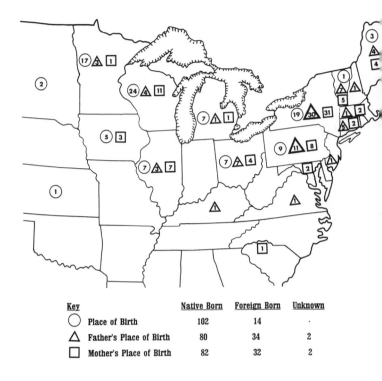

Key		Native Born	Foreign Born	Unknown
○	Place of Birth	102	14	·
△	Father's Place of Birth	80	34	2
□	Mother's Place of Birth	82	32	2

Sources of migration to De Smet, 1880. *(Map drawn by Orville Gab)*

state forms a transitional area and that its northern sections contributed to the Yankee migration. Minnesota also ranked high as a place of birth in 1880, because many of the young children in De Smet had been born there before the families moved to Dakota Territory.

Few adults had been born in Minnesota or anywhere else in the Midwest; for the most part, they had been born east of Ohio or in a foreign country. Perusing the place-of-birth columns in the census records produces a picture of a leapfrogging sort of migration to the west.[13] Sometimes people jumped directly from an eastern state to Dakota Territory, but census records for 1900 to 1920 more often show families moving west step-by-step, as they traced routes through Ohio, Illinois, Wisconsin, Iowa, Minnesota, and the surrounding states. In families with eight or ten children, we can get a notion of step-migration across the continent by observing the birth places of the different children. Of the eighteen married couples in De Smet in 1880, one had three children, two had four, and the rest had two or fewer. The Ingalls girls—Mary, Laura, Carrie, and Grace—had been born in Wisconsin, Kansas, and Iowa, and the parents had been born in New York and Wisconsin. The Woodworth boys—James, Benjamin (he has a birthday party in *Little Town on the Prairie*), Walter, and Richard—had been born in Michigan, Illinois, Wisconsin, and Illinois again while their parents had been born in Ohio and Illinois. The children of the Beardsleys (whose hotel is mentioned in *The Long Winter* and *Little Town on the Prairie*) —Walter, James, and Mary—had been born in Wisconsin and Dakota Territory, their parents in New York and Wisconsin.[14] The records show a westward drift of migration even though families like the Ingallses and the Woodworths jumped back and forth in their movements.

It would be fascinating to trace the origins and the exact routes of the families who came to De Smet during the early 1880s, but we must be content, for the most part, with noting their states or countries of birth as recorded in the census. Sometimes, though, other biographical facts can be gleaned from obituaries, newspaper stories, and personal accounts. One Zoa Moran Sturgeon, for example, was born in Quebec in 1841 and moved with her husband to Austin, Minnesota, in 1869. Nine years later the family moved further west to Marshall, Minnesota, and then in the fall of 1882 they took over a hotel business in De Smet, Dakota Territory. Mrs. Sturgeon lived there the last thirty-four years of her life.

Another example of a westward-moving migrant who wound up permanently in De Smet was Charleton S. G. Fuller, who was born in Bath, England, in 1847. When he was about thirteen, he emigrated to the United States with his parents, settling in the vicinity of Syracuse, New York. After engaging for some time in business in Chicago, he formed a partnership with Andrew Dox and opened a hardware store in Brookings, Dakota Territory, the year it was established in 1879. The following year he moved forty miles further along the railroad to the new town of De Smet, where he lived for another quarter century, dying there in 1905 at the age of fifty-seven.[15] Fuller—referred to in the books as Gerald Fuller—was the hardware man in a store across Main Street from the Ingalls building, and his store was a gathering place for people during the long winter.

Based on census information alone, we can see that De Smet was a destination in the stream of migration that flowed across the northern part of the country, originating in the Yankee and, to a lesser degree, the Midland cultural hearths. Almost no De Smetites came from the South, and only tiny numbers arrived from the border states. However, the originating sources of the settlers moved constantly westward as time went by. Later there would be small delegations from states further west—California and Montana—but by the early 1900s, the predominant places of birth of De Smet residents were Wisconsin, Iowa, Minnesota, and Illinois (aside from South Dakota itself).[16]

If the Yankee migration set the tone for the town's character, a generous sprinkling of foreign-born and second-generation immigrants leavened the mixture. Although only 14 of the town's 116 residents in the 1880 census were foreign born, 22 others were native born with at least one foreign-born parent. Most of those parents had come from Canada or the British Isles, but one or two parents in each case were from Norway, Denmark, Germany, and France. Later on, the number of residents with Scandinavian or German backgrounds increased in comparison to those with English or Irish backgrounds.[17]

The proportion of first- and second-generation immigrants in town resembled the proportion in the countryside, which runs counter to a common stereotype in the Midwest of Yankee storekeepers and immigrant farmers. Only eight adult foreign-born males lived in De Smet in

1880, and little of significance can be concluded from looking at their occupations. The three Canadians were a butcher, a farmer, and a grocer; the two Danes were railroad laborers; the two Scots were a farmer and a carpenter; the Norwegian was a railroad laborer. Of the fourteen adult males born in the United States whose fathers had been born abroad, the seven who were of English stock were an agricultural implement dealer, the clerk of the district court, a hardware dealer, a lawyer, a hostler, a shoemaker, and a tinsmith; the three of Irish background were a land agent, a lumber dealer, and a railroad laborer; the Frenchman was a grain dealer; the Scot was a blacksmith; the Canadian was a farmer; and the Prussian was a printer. No broad generalizations are possible from these figures except that there was no observable tendency for immigrants to be channeled into lower-status occupations.

The most obvious characteristic of this population on the edge of the agricultural frontier was its youth.[18] The average age (mean, 25.9; median, 27) was not particularly low, largely because there were not enough children to counterbalance a number of young, single males. The numbers of both younger and older people were relatively small in the beginning, making for an unusual age pyramid. The population consisted largely of young adults, most of whom, as was typical of the early years on the frontier, were male. Close to half (43.1 percent) of the townspeople were in their twenties, and almost two-thirds (64.7 percent) were between twenty-one and forty years old. Males in their twenties outnumbered females two to one; for those in their thirties the ratio was four to one. Had the census taker arrived a year or two or even a month or two later, the age breakdown and the gender ratio would have been less skewed, as more and larger families continued to arrive.[19] Husbands frequently preceded their wives and families to new locations on the frontier, starting a homestead or a business and returning home during the winter to bring their wives and families back the following spring. In addition to the eighteen husband-wife couples that were counted in De Smet in 1880, seven other married adult males lived there without their wives; two of them had sons in their twenties living with them.

How many of these families and single migrants came to the Dakota frontier to stay, and how many of them would move on to other places? Everywhere on the edge of settlement there was a considerable churning of the population, as many individuals and families stayed only a short time in one place and then moved on to greener pastures. If some of the founding families in a community remained for generations, more of the early arrivals stayed for only a short time. De Smet proved to be no exception to this rule. Examining the federal census manuscripts for the town of De Smet from 1880 and 1900 (the ones from 1890 were destroyed in a fire), only 20 percent of the heads of household who were registered in the former were still present at the time of the latter. The persistence rate of heads of household in De Smet between 1900 and 1910 was 30.8 percent (but since about ten of them probably died during the decade, a figure of about 36 percent is more realistic).

Impressionistic observations from the De Smet *Leader* and other sources suggest that many of the early arrivals, such as Robert Boast and Charles H. Tinkham, stayed in De Smet or in the area for decades. Charles Ingalls was one of those persisters. Another early arrival was Charles E. Ely, a veteran of the Battle of Gettysburg and a lumber dealer in town, who stayed on for three-and-a-half decades before seeking relief from health problems in Texas and Hot Springs, South Dakota, shortly before his death.[20] Frank Schaub, an early-day harnessmaker, ran a clothing store in De Smet for many years, selling out his stock in 1925 when he became county register of deeds.[21] L. E. Sasse, who built a number of grain elevators in towns along the railroad before becoming the agent of the Scofield elevator in De Smet, later operated a drugstore from 1884 until his death in 1906. Christian Lyngbye, an early-day blacksmith, lived in town until he died in 1921.[22]

E. H. Couse served as the first president of the Kingsbury County Illinois Association after it started up in 1910. When he died in 1916, his funeral was held in the opera house that he had built on the second floor of his new brick hardware store in 1886. His few remaining comrades from the Civil War joined his fellow businessmen, neighbors, and friends to bid him farewell. Born in New York State, Couse had been a Republican ever since the party's founding and had actively participated for years in the temperance movement. Of this quintessential Yankee storekeeper, newspaper editor Carter Sherwood (who had arrived in town in 1883 and who, with his son Aubrey, edited the newspaper for more than nine decades) simply noted: "Columns could be written laudatory of the good deeds of our honored citizen, but to what end? His life was an open book, and his acquaintances know what we know. Strangers are not interested."[23]

Probably the most prominent businessman in town during its first half century of existence was Daniel Loftus, who arrived in town as a twenty-eight-year-old Pennsylvanian of Irish background. He was listed in the 1880 census as a land agent who boarded at one of the hotels on Calumet Avenue. Laura Ingalls Wilder immortalized him in *The Long Winter* as the storekeeper who tried to profit from the sale of the wheat that Almanzo and Cap had risked their lives to get in order to save the starving townspeople,[24] but in later years Loftus must have done right by his customers because he prospered and went on to local and statewide prominence. After a stint as vice-president of the South Dakota Retail Merchants Association he became its president, and when a commercial club was established in town in 1907, he was also elected as its first president. Not only did Loftus remain in town until he died in 1921, but his gravestone was the biggest one in the De Smet cemetery—and still is.[25]

So there were the stayers, but there also were a considerable number of people for whom De Smet and its rural countryside were merely way stations on their paths to the West Coast or elsewhere. Especially notable were the large number who jumped all the way to California, Washington, Oregon, and even Alaska. Laura Brown, the widow of former De Smet *Leader* coeditor Mark Brown, wrote from her home in San Diego in February 1922 to describe a South Dakota picnic she had recently attended at Mission Cliff Gardens near her home. She reported that about six hundred people attended, including at least two others from Kingsbury County.[26]

One of the people who read about this event in the paper was Jake Hopp, the newspaper editor who had sold Laura Ingalls her namecards in *Little Town on the Prairie*. He had arrived in De Smet as a twenty-two-year-old bachelor in 1880, when he drove out with a team and wagon with Brookings lawyer George A. Mathews to start the Kingsbury County *News*. After 1883 there were two newspapers in town, providing some competition, and in 1890 Jake Hopp sold out his interest in the *News* and lit out for the West—in this case Bellingham, Washington, where he continued in the newspaper trade while also engaging in the hardware business. The frontier spirit carried his brother George, an editor in Brookings, even further; after spending some time in Washington he moved all the way to Alaska.[27]

One of the most attractive destinations for former South Dakotans during the early 1900s was the Los Angeles area, where a huge South Dakota picnic became a yearly event. A. E. Carpenter, a longtime De Smet grocer who later lived in Mitchell for a short time, jumped all the way out to Pomona in 1921 and started a business there. Dr. L. F. Straight practiced dentistry in De Smet from the early 1880s until failing health led him to move to Pasadena in 1918, where he lived until his death in 1926. Dr. Sidney Broadbent, who spent part of his childhood in De Smet, where his father was a business partner of Daniel Loftus, moved with his family first to Minnesota and then to California. He developed a private medical practice in Hollywood and was holding a chair in the Los Angeles College of Medicine when he made visits back to his old hometown during the early 1920s.[28]

Chicago and Minneapolis were also popular destinations for former De Smetites. Visscher V. Barnes, the lawyer who gave the firecrackers to Pa Ingalls to give to his girls at the July Fourth celebration in *Little Town on the Prairie*, played a significant role in territorial politics and the temperance movement before moving to Zion, Illinois, north of Chicago. He stayed in touch with people from his old hometown, writing letters to the newspaper from time to time to reminisce about the early days, and in a letter to Carter Sherwood in 1922, two years before his death, Barnes noted that many of his old Dakota friends were living in Chicago, including A. B. Melville, formerly of Huron, who was a leading attorney in the city.[29]

Anecdotal evidence of this type suggests the importance of migration in the lives of people who were among the early residents of De Smet. The general pattern of out-migration found graphic portrayal in a series of lists published in 1917 in the De Smet *News*. Editor Carter Sherwood, who had come to town in 1883 and therefore probably knew almost everyone who had ever lived there, invited people to send in names and addresses of people who had moved away. By the time he was through, he had accumulated a list of approximately three hundred names and addresses (in most cases, just the name of the town and the state were mentioned). In 1921, Sherwood ran addresses again. Most of these were duplications of the ones that had run four years earlier, but in some cases people had moved again. There were also about fifty new names added to the list.[30]

By mapping out these locations, we can get a good indication of how dispersed the population was and where former De Smetites went after leaving town. A breakdown, by state and Canadian province, listed below includes towns or cities that had three or more people listed:

Location of Former Residents, 1917–1921

Arizona	1
Arkansas	2

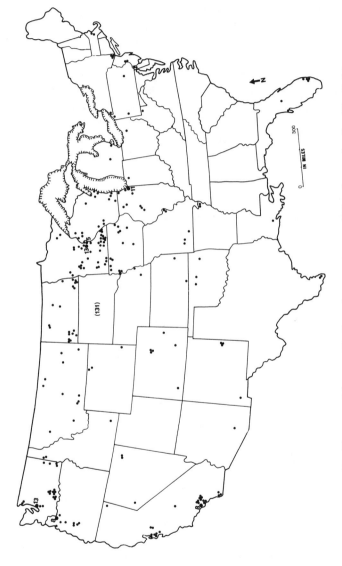

(131)

13

13

N

0   300
IN MILES

Residences of former De Smetites, 1917–1921. *(Map drawn by Orville Gab)*

California	34	Los Angeles, 8; Pomona, 4; Long Beach, 3; Pasadena, 3; San Jose, 3; Santa Monica, 3
Colorado	6	Denver, 3
Delaware	2	
Florida	7	Delray, 3
Hawaii	1	
Idaho	5	
Illinois	19	Chicago, 11
Indiana	2	
Iowa	16	Sioux City, 3
Kansas	2	
Louisiana	1	
Massachusetts	2	
Michigan	3	
Minnesota	57	Minneapolis, 13; St. Paul, 5; Stewartville, 3; Winona, 3
Mississippi	1	
Missouri	5	
Montana	18	
Nebraska	2	
Nevada	3	
New Jersey	3	
New Mexico	4	Melrose, 3
New York	6	New York City, 3
North Dakota	24	Beach, 3; Lisbon, 3
Ohio	2	
Oklahoma	3	
Oregon	16	Portland, 8
Pennsylvania	5	
South Dakota	131	
Texas	2	
West Virginia	1	
Washington	35	Seattle, 13; Zillah, 4; Toppenish, 3; Yakima, 3
Wisconsin	16	
Wyoming	7	

Alberta, Can.	3		
Manitoba	1		
Ontario	1		
Saskatchewan	1		

Towns in South Dakota with 3 or more listed

Aberdeen	11	Sioux Falls	13
Brookings	8	Vermillion	6
Highmore	4	Watertown	7
Hurley	4	Willow Lake	3
Huron	5	Wolsey	3
Lake Preston	5	Yankton	3
Oldham	3		

People who moved to other places in South Dakota constituted by far the largest group of out-migrants. They may have been overrepresented because, being nearby, they were more likely to remain in touch with friends and relatives and to send in their addresses. On the other hand, they may have been underrepresented because people may not have bothered to send their names and addresses to the editor since they lived so close by. Outside South Dakota, Minnesota had the largest number of out-migrants. The Twin Cities area, with eighteen former De Smetites, ranked with the Los Angeles area as home to the largest number. Especially striking was the large number who settled in the three West Coast states. Los Angeles, Long Beach, and surrounding communities were strong magnets for De Smetites and their fellow South Dakotans during the early 1900s. Only slightly less attractive were the Seattle, Washington, and Portland, Oregon, areas. San Francisco and its environs also attracted a number of people.[31] Wisconsin, Iowa, North Dakota, and Montana also harbored large numbers of former De Smetites, and Illinois' total was swelled by the eleven who settled in Chicago. Fewer De Smet residents moved east of Chicago, the most notable exceptions being three in New York City and seven in Florida, including the John Carroll family.

Generalizing from these observations, we can say that from a relatively early date, many De Smetites pushed all the way to the West Coast, and even larger numbers got caught up in the churning migration in the Midwest. Relatively few bounced back further east than Chicago, and, except for Florida, southern states seemed to be unattractive to them.

One person who did not make it onto editor Sherwood's lists was Rose Wilder Lane, who had grown up with her parents at Rocky Ridge Farm near Mansfield, Missouri. In 1915, the forty-eight-year-old Laura Ingalls Wilder took a train out to visit her daughter in San Francisco, where she was working for the San Francisco *Bulletin*. Lane apparently found it hard to settle down in one place. After divorcing her husband Gillette Lane, she traveled frequently around the United States, Europe, and the Near East, and she lived at various times in Paris, back in Mansfield, in New York City, and in Danbury, Connecticut.[32] Like her mother and her grandfather, she seemed, for a while at least, to have that "itchy foot" that drove people to keep moving.

A look at the in-migrants and out-migrants of Wilder's "little town on the prairie" reminds us that for many people De Smet was not the end of the line in the pioneering process. Although it is not invalid to see the migratory stream that the Ingalls family was caught up in as part of Frederick Jackson Turner's frontier process, it is more useful to think of the paths that led to and from the town as part of the broader churning phenomenon that George W. Pierson has referred to as the M factor in American history.

9 / Relaxing and Building Community at the Couse Opera House

Laura Ingalls Wilder's novels are filled with such joy and delight that the reader is tempted at times to forget just how dull small prairie towns were. Little railroad towns like De Smet were established by the Chicago and North Western Railroad to funnel commodities produced by farmers who lived along its line to distant markets. Their original purpose was economic, but as soon as the towns were established, they took on other functions—social, political, and cultural. Once the storekeepers, grain elevator operators, lumber dealers, and other businessmen and their families arrived in a new town to make a living, they also had to make a life for themselves. That involved the formation of schools, churches, eating places, lodge halls, pool rooms, ball diamonds, saloons (in places where liquor was legal), and, inevitably, opera houses.

Every town of any pretension whatsoever (and that included most) got its opera house within a few years, and for decades the building served as a community center, bringing the populace together for traveling entertainments, local talent shows, political speeches, temperance rallies, Decoration Day services, New Year's dances, roller-skating, school graduations, and public meetings, depending on what the hall could accommodate and what the people in the locality demanded.[1]

De Smet was without an opera house until the end of 1886, and for the first seven years of the town's existence, people had to rely on other rooms and buildings for the kinds of activities that would later take place in the opera

Company E in parade formation in front of the Couse Opera House. *(Courtesy South Dakota State Historical Society)*

house. These were the years that Laura Ingalls wrote about in her last four novels. When she and Almanzo got married in August 1885, at the end of *These Happy Golden Years*, the "hot spot" for entertainment in De Smet was a roller rink that had been built the previous year. Not until December 1886—the month that Rose was born—was the newly dedicated Couse Opera House ready for its first function, a supper and bazaar put on by the Baptist ladies aid.[2]

Since newspapers do not survive from the first three years of De Smet's existence, our knowledge of the earliest town activities is limited. But beginning in January 1883, the paragraph items about local events in the De Smet *Leader*, provide a rather detailed view of the kinds of social events that occurred, though there are major gaps in the collection of papers covering the later years. The very first issue of De Smet's second newspaper noted the need for a good public hall. "Here is an opportunity for some enterprising citizen to distinguish himself and confer a lasting benefit upon the community," editor Mark Brown observed. He reiterated the theme in April: "Of all the wants of De Smet the most urgent is a public hall. Who will erect it and immortalize himself?" And again in December: "Our need of a public hall becomes more apparent constantly. Where is our public spirited citizen?"[3]

In the absence of an opera house or public hall, De Smetites followed the example of people in other towns who were in similar circumstances—they gathered in any room or building they could use or commandeer, usually in a church or a schoolhouse. The school, on the north side of Second Street two blocks west of Calumet Avenue, was small and could not accommodate more than several dozen people at the most. Built soon after the town was established, the school soon outlived its purpose and was replaced in November 1884 with a new $5,000 grade school built a couple of blocks west of the old one. Meanwhile, kitty-corner south across Second Street sat the town's first church, which the Congregationalists generously shared with the Baptists and the Methodists until the latter two congregations were able to erect their own edifices in 1884 and 1885. The fourth denomination in town, the Catholics, moved their services out of the schoolhouse and into their own new building in the fall of 1883, only to have it blown down in a wind storm the following August.[4]

Before the roller rink was constructed, the Congregational church remained the most active community meeting center in town, and even after the rink opened, it was frequently used. Typical of the kinds of entertainment offered there in 1883 was a performance by Professor James G. Clark, a singer and poet who delighted a small audience (small because of an unannounced change of date). Another professor (this one named Morris), who was identified as a graduate of Fowler and Wells' Institute, offered free public examinations to entice people to his phrenological lectures, which were illustrated ''by a large collection of pictures and eight human skulls.'' After the first evening's performance, which was free, admission to the next two evenings' entertainments was ten cents. His readings of Messrs. Ely and Carroll caused ''uproarious fun.'' Then S. B. Owen and Elder Annes submitted to examination, causing further amusement on the part of the audience. A stereopticon show also attracted a full house, affording ''quite creditable amusement.''[5]

People in towns like De Smet wanted to relax and to be entertained when they attended these gatherings, and they generally found what they were looking for. Local talent frequently was tapped for sociables and musical entertainments at the churches. Everybody in town, whatever his or her denomination, was invited to Sunday School concerts. New England (often, baked-bean) suppers were popular, and ice cream socials, often linked with strawberries, were another favorite.[6]

Before the rink or the opera house became available for traveling entertainments, churches served as venues for these performances. Donavin's Original Tennesseeans received a warm reception in the new Baptist church in November 1884, and Hagerman, the troupe's wonderful basso, ''brought down the house frequently,'' it was reported in the paper. The Stewart Grand Concert Company visited De Smet in the spring of 1886 and returned in October to perform in the Congregational church. Their six members included a pianist, a soprano (advertised as one who ''has a rich, sweet voice, and carries her audience to the verge of ecstasy''), a contralto, a tenor, a basso (''Thunder itself is the only thing we can name that in the least approximates the sounds this man sends forth without an effort''), and an elocutionist (''a whole show in himself'').[7]

Complementing such entertainments was a variety of educational and uplifting lectures and performances. In a town with no public library and few books or other kinds of reading material in people's homes outside of some newspapers and magazines, many people were hungry for ideas and information, especially if they were packaged in easily digestible and entertaining form. Rev. Edward Brown's speaking style apparently exerted a more positive effect on many people than it did on young Laura Ingalls, who found it repelling. His series of geological lectures at the Congregational church in the fall of 1883, for the purpose of raising funds to pay for a bell for the church, aroused "great interest" in his audiences if the newspaper can be believed. Four years later he gave another series of six lectures on the same subject.[8]

The Baptists were favored in November 1885 with a lecture on the city of Washington by E. T. Cressey of Huron, who had served there for several years as a clerk in the House of Representatives. A few weeks later, at the Congregational church, Hon. G. C. Williams "held the close attention of his entire audience" with a lecture on the "Ins and Outs of Congress." In April 1887, the wife of Thomas L. Riggs of the Oahe Indian Mission gave a lecture at the church on her and her husband's missionary activities. Later that summer, the Methodist church was the scene for Minneapolis pastor John Stafford's entertaining lecture on "A Trip to Venice," and a few months later Professor Wakefield of Dakota University, the Methodist school in Mitchell, gave a lecture on "True Manliness."[9]

For many decades thereafter, the churches provided meeting places for their own congregations and for the entire community, hosting union revival meetings, chicken pie suppers, stereopticon entertainments, baccalaureate services, Christmas Eve exercises, high school debates, violin solos, bazaars, cantatas, father-and-son and mother-and-daughter banquets, and other kinds of activities.[10] An editorial in the De Smet *News* in 1943 commented on church socials:

> There has been much said and written about public dinners being overdone by the churches, and the criticism has some merit. Yet they have their part in community life, making a pleasant gathering for the pub-

lic. I thought of it Sunday, as folks from over a wide area patronized the St. Patrick's dinner at the St. Thomas church. There was plenty of visiting going on while waiting for tables, and during the very good meal served by the altar society.[11]

During the first several years of De Smet's existence, the schoolhouse was the other major community gathering place, although once the Congregational church was available, it, and later the other churches, probably took over most of the community gatherings because of the small size of the school. The schoolhouse most likely was largely confined to school events and other educational gatherings. For example, in March 1886 there was a debate on the question of whether to divide Dakota Territory and immediately seek admission into the Union for the southern half. Participating in the discussion were Charles H. Tinkham, John H. Carroll, Visscher V. Barnes, Charles E. Ely, and G. W. Elliott. De Smetites also held a social there that fall to get acquainted with the teachers and a spelling bee like the one described by Laura Ingalls Wilder in *Little Town on the Prairie*.[12]

After the turn of the century, and especially after about 1910, school activities increasingly occupied front-row-center in town life. The high school band took over the role earlier filled by militia and cornet bands, and high school plays likewise superseded local talent shows. By the 1920s high school athletics emerged as a major diversion and subject of discussion in the community. Baseball was established in De Smet during the early 1900s, and basketball got started around 1907. Basketball games were first played on an outdoor court at the Athletic Park, which made weather a factor during the first couple years, but they soon moved into the opera house, and then, sometime during the middle teens, they were switched over to the Floto Auditorium located in the building next door. The auditorium, a large hall used for dances, movies, and other entertainments, seemed adequate for a while. But during the early 1920s, as neighboring towns built new brick high schools and included gymnasiums in them, De Smetites began to feel the need for a new playing facility of their own. Their own school addition, built in 1922, lacked the sizable playing facility many townspeople thought they needed. Not until the construction of a large new gymnasium in 1938 did the town catch up with many of its nearby rivals.[13]

The wide variety of social and cultural activities available in De Smet from its very beginning—particularly those devoted to amusement and self-improvement—reflected a common impulse in small midwestern towns. Late-nineteenth-century migrants from New York and New England began trying to re-create their familiar society and culture as soon as they arrived in the Midwest, but their geographical remoteness from Chicago, New York, and Boston—and even Minneapolis and Omaha—remained a fact of life. Nevertheless, the rough edges of frontier existence soon were moderated by a wide assortment of educational and recreational activities that reflected people's aspirations to respectability and cultivation.[14]

Literary societies and study groups appealed to many. At a literary society meeting in the De Smet Congregational church in February 1883, H. G. Woodworth's select reading was followed by a debate on the topic, "Resolved: That the expenses of the U. S. government should be met by direct taxation." Graham and Whiting took the affirmative side, Couse and Thomas the negative. Either the debate was short or the meeting was long, because after a recess and a musical number, John H. Carroll did a reading and Rev. Edward Brown gave a lecture, which was followed by more music and final adjournment. During the winter of 1886, a literary society called the De Smet Reading Circle met weekly from January through April. Musical selections, prose and poetry readings, biographical sketches, and critiques of authors' styles focused on Sir Walter Scott, Washington Irving, J. G. Holland, and other popular authors. The programs attracted many of the town's leading figures, including R. A. Cashman, J. F. Watson, John

A. Owen, J. B. Hall, Visscher V. Barnes, V. S. L. Owen, G. W. Elliott, C. S. G. Fuller, C. J. Thomas, Carter P. Sherwood, G. A. Williams, E. F. Barrows, and their wives.[15]

An effort to start a local Chautauqua Literary and Scientific Circle in De Smet in 1885 apparently fizzled.[16] That same year an entertainment series (educational and entertainment programs or courses frequently went under the title of "Lyceum series")was held in De Smet, but such programs did not become a regular feature in town until after the turn of the century.[17] Other types of entertainments, some formal and some informal, also provided diversion for De Smet's citizenry. Seasonal activities included hunting and fishing, ice skating and sledding, swimming, and other sports, such as baseball, tennis, and golf. From the days of Wilder's girlhood on into the 1920s, skating on Silver Lake was a popular pastime, and picnics, dances, and sociables of various kinds were also common. During the first several years of the town's existence, the hotels were also social centers for games of checkers, oyster suppers, taffy pulls, and other activities.[18]

Baseball teams were perennial attractions and barometers of community pride, and early-day baseball games tended to be high-scoring affairs. For instance, the De Smet Clippers defeated the nearby town of Nordland, 57 to 11, in a game in August 1883; three years later they lost a game to the same team, 30 to 5. Another De Smet town baseball team, the White Stockings, defeated Lake Preston's team by scores of 36 to 21 and 45 to 43 in 1886.[19]

Clubs and organizations—from the Grand Army of the Republic (GAR) to a hook-and-ladder team to ladies aids and the Women's Christian Temperance Union—provided outlets for male and female, young and old. The GAR had its auxiliary, the Women's Relief Corps, as did many of the fraternal lodges. The Masons, the Odd Fellows, and the Ancient Order of United Woodmen all got early starts in De Smet, and an agricultural society to organize the county fair was also established early.

Clearly, then, there was no lack of activities in De Smet. Yet without an opera house, De Smet was a poor relation in comparison to its neighbors. The precursor to the opera house was the roller rink that opened for business in August 1884, an event reported by the De Smet *Leader*: "The band hall is being revamped into a skating rink, and the grand promenade is expected to open the middle of next week." After a couple of weeks of operation, the band members, who still owned the building, put in a hardwood floor for better skating. The band usually played for the skaters one of the two or three evenings a week that the rink was open, and it also played for dances and other entertainments. An orchestra also started up around 1886.[20]

The opening of the rink coincided with a roller-skating craze that was spreading across the country and into Dakota Territory by the summer and fall of 1884. Every town, it seems, had to have its own rink. In "Pioneer Girl," Laura admitted that one day she had played hookey from school with other children and gone skating at the rink. Besides regular skating, racing exhibitions became a regular feature in the hall.

Although pictures of the building do not survive, a room large enough to accommodate skaters as well as a stage that could be used for the band or other entertainers certainly would have provided a better venue for traveling road shows than any other building in De Smet. Mayne's Minstrels, who arrived toward the end of April 1885, were probably the first touring group to perform in the rink. Miss Jones, an elocutionist, followed in their wake. A male quartet called the Nashville Students appeared in October. A local talent group from Arlington, twenty miles down the railroad tracks, played "War to the Knife" the following spring. The Stewart concert troupe, a group of black singers, came in May. Several other entertainments were given, and a political rally was held at the rink before the opera house opened in late 1886. Immediately thereafter, the band association disposed of the rink to L. E. Fellows, who turned it into a machinery warehouse.[21]

After several years of hearing it said that some conscientious citizen should assume the task of building a public hall, Edward H. Couse decided to take the initiative. Couse, born in 1830 in Otsego County in east-central New York State, had moved with his family to Illinois when he was fourteen and later went to Minnesota as a young man. He moved out to Volga at the end of the line in 1879 and the following year followed the tracklayers to De Smet as the railroad extended west. A Civil War veteran, he remained active in GAR activities, participated in the De Smet veterans unit, and frequently attended campfires in nearby towns. He had purchased his lot and the original store building on it from Charles P. Ingalls, who retained his other store kitty-corner from it at the intersection of Main and Second streets.[22] Like many of his fellow businessmen, Couse played an active role in the community and in 1887 took a position on the city council, serving as street commissioner. Partly as an encouragement to his fellow residents to plant trees on their property, he planted some on the courthouse square in 1890. Couse also assumed the position of secretary of the new De Smet Cheese and Butter Company, whose meetings were frequently held in his store.[23]

By 1885 Couse had succeeded well enough with his hardware business to expand his operation and replace his original wood-frame building (popularly known as the "Old Reliable") with a new brick-veneered store building on the 50-foot frontage of lots eight and nine of block one. Except for a couple of banks, his new building immediately became—and remains today—the most impressive business structure on Main Street. Almost every town like De Smet went through several phases in which the original false-front wooden structures were replaced by larger buildings of brick or stone, then eventually even these were torn down or renovated to make way for more modern structures. Couse started the process in De Smet with his decision to build. Simultaneously, the two bankers in town—John H. Carroll and Thomas H. Ruth—decided to construct new brick bank buildings.

Originally, Couse had planned to build in early 1885, but

something led him to postpone going ahead with his plan for a year. In January 1886, he journeyed to Sioux Falls to consult an architect and then went to Minneapolis to let the contract. He instead returned home and decided to be his own general contractor. The old building was moved off the lot in April, and work began. Built during the summer of 1886, the new edifice, which cost about $9,000, was a 44-foot by 80-foot brick-veneered structure with two stories and a basement. Galvanized iron trim typical of the time lent the building dignity, even if it could not aspire to the impressiveness of stores in larger cities. In bold letters set on the cornice crowning the building were the words, "Couse Block."[24]

The first floor was divided into three rooms—a hardware salesroom on the left as one entered the store, 22 feet wide and running the entire 80-foot length of the building; another 22-foot salesroom (for stoves and heavy hardware) on the right, going back for 60 feet; and a small tin shop behind the second room that extended back another 20 feet toward the alley. The ceilings were 12 feet high, and the salesrooms were finished in cherry and black walnut stain. An elevator at the back of the building, running down to the basement and up to the second floor, was available for moving furniture, stored inventory, heavy machinery, and props and scenery used by traveling troupes who played in the opera house.[25]

Upstairs was the grand opera hall: 44 feet wide and 60 feet long, with the stage extending back another 18 feet. It was plastered, and the casings were painted in light and dark blue. In October, just as the brick veneer was being completed, Couse made a trip to Chicago to order three hundred portable opera chairs to use in the hall, and he also purchased a full set of curtains for the stage. The room was entered by a broad stairway on the north side of the building, and in the entryway there was a ticket office and a cloakroom. Now the community could rightfully take pride in itself.[26] Except for Huron, thirty-five miles to the west, De Smet now possessed the finest opera house on its stretch of railroad through eastern Dakota Territory, although Brookings and Pierre would later outdo the De Smet hall when they built their new facilities in 1904 and 1906.

Couse was not content merely to announce the completion of his new store building and the opening of the opera house and planned an elaborate dedication ceremony, the likes of which had never been seen in the town. Intending to make his new hall "essentially a public institution," he invited not only the entire population of De Smet but people in communities all around to attend the festivities on the evening of November 11, 1886. A general reception at 8 o'clock featured music by the De Smet Orchestra and the Choral Union. In his welcoming remarks, proprietor Couse announced that the hall would be available free of charge for use by religious and civic organizations, a generous gesture which elicited cheers from the audience. After Amos Whiting recalled the history of the construction of the new building, with references also to the two new bank structures in town, toastmaster Alfred Thomas called for brief comments on the community and its progress from a number of prominent local residents: Rev. Edward Brown ("De Smet between 1880 and 1886"), John A. Owen ("De Smet Opera House"), Rev. G. D. Ballantine ("Our Host and Hostess"), V. S. L. Owen ("Our Ladies"), Philip Lawrence ("Our Commerce"), Charles H. Tinkham ("Our Game"), J. B. Hall ("Our Dogs"), Rev. F. H. Wheeler ("Our Schools"), and John H. Carroll ("The Future of De Smet").[27]

Topping off the ceremony was a wedding, performed by Justice S. B. Owen. In announcing the big shindig two-and-a-half weeks earlier, Couse had offered to present the first couple to "have the courage to get married at this reception" a splendid new cookstove and outfit. Had the opportunity occurred a year earlier, the lucky couple might have been Laura Ingalls and Almanzo Wilder, but this evening it was Edward A. Bornemann and Emma Comstock, who obtained the elegant cookstove and a "small load of tinware" for their part in the entertainment. "The cheers that followed the ceremony were loud and long," the De Smet *Leader* reported.

Refreshments were served to 250 people in the rooms below at 10:30. Soon the dancing started, with Dan Collins calling, and 140 couples took part. Meanwhile, over at the Howland Hotel about 150 couples took their supper. "Not until nearly daylight did the dancing cease and the tired participants depart," the newspaper observed. "To say the whole entertainment was a success is putting it but mildly. It will long be remembered by everyone present."

A barber shop with shower bath was soon installed in the basement, and because De Smet had no courthouse at the time, another section of the basement was fixed up to serve as a courtroom. In short order the opera house became the center of community activities and remained so for more than two decades. A program on Christmas night with songs and recitations brought out an estimated five hundred people, and the children were all presented with little sacks of sweetmeats. The Catholics held a supper and dance there in January, which was followed by a masquerade ball sponsored by the Select Knights of the Ancient Order of United Woodmen. The band was soon practicing in the opera house on Saturday nights, and cooperative religious services were held there on Sunday evenings.[28]

The first dramatic entertainment in the new opera house was put on by Ford's Dramatic Company on Thursday, Friday, and Saturday, January 3–5, 1887. The troupe, made up of fifteen players, put on a street parade during the afternoon to announce its presence. The full house that turned out for the performance of "Phoenix" on opening night was reported by the *Leader* as highly appreciative of the effort. But Friday evening's rendition of "Joshua Whitcomb," a sentimental story about bygone days in New England that had become a staple with traveling troupes during the period, was unappreciated by at least one member of the audience. Although it was widely popular wherever it was shown and called by Eugene Field "altogether the best American play yet produced," the play was termed outrageous in a letter written to the *Leader*. Admitting that the music was good and the acting fair, the agitated theater-goer condemned the play's "downright vulgarity and obscenity, to say nothing of sickly attempts at profanity." The editor dutifully published the long letter, which complained that, "we cannot think we live in an atmosphere so like that of ancient Sodom and Gomorrah."[29]

Protecting the morals of the citizenry was always of concern to community leaders, and traveling entertainment companies frequently emphasized the clean and wholesome nature of their shows in the advertising they used, although some of their programs in fact verged on suggestiveness and indecency, at least as they were interpreted at the time. Then, as now, ambiguous messages were often sent by entertainers, who wanted to titillate without offending too much. Criticisms aimed at performances, however, were usually concerned less with taste than with competence. Towns the size of De Smet tended to be visited by second- or third-rung theater companies, so people especially appreciated it when a really first-class crew came to town and frequently complained about downright bad singers and actors. "The worst imposition ever practiced on De Smet in the show line" was the judgment rendered a stereopticon entertainment by Dill Brothers and Company in March 1887.[30]

More often, however, the notices were positive. People welcomed chances to alleviate the monotony of small-town life and to get out of the house, and it was a real treat to attend a well-acted play or to hear a good violinist or soprano vocalist. Local talent, though not necessarily bad, could seldom match the professionals who arrived by train to perform at the opera house. Farm families drove in from the countryside, when the weather was good, and for headline companies people often traveled by rail from nearby towns to attend performances.

When the Andrews Opera Company performed *The Mikado* in May 1887, George Andrews may have exaggerated slightly in calling the Couse Opera House the best hall to sing in that his group had experienced in the territory, but local folks were quick to welcome this talented crew whenever it came to town. That month also witnessed the first of many performances in De Smet of *Uncle Tom's Cabin*, which was performed across the United States during the late 1800s and early 1900s by hundreds of companies.[31] After taking in performances by the John Dillon Company, Puck's Comedy Company, Gee's Lilliputian Band, the McGibeny family, the Slayton Tennesseeans, D. R. Willson, Axel Skovgaard, and dozens of others, De Smetites felt they were beginning to enjoy the kind of cultural climate they had been familiar with back East.[32]

The two most popular groups to perform in De Smet over the years were probably the Lawrence Deming Theatre Company and Clint and Bessie Robbins and their entourage. Deming's twelve-person company played to a full house during their first three-night engagement in February 1916 and were warmly welcomed back whenever they returned during the next several years. "The Demings will always draw a good house in De Smet," the De Smet *News* warmly observed.[33] But no doubt the greatest attraction ever to visit the area was Clint and Bessie Robbins, who were well known for their performances around the Midwest. Though their company had previously confined its playing in South Dakota to larger towns like Watertown, Aberdeen, and Huron, De Smet was written into the schedule in December 1918, when a flu epidemic forced the cancellation of its dates in Brookings. By this time, many performances had moved over from the Couse Opera House into the newer Floto Auditorium in the building next door. The following spring the Robbins company was back for another week's engagement at the Floto. When they played in Huron in 1926, many De Smetites drove over to watch them, but efforts to bring them back to De Smet failed because they "were booked up." However, "Clint and Bessie," as folks affectionately referred to them, did come back to perform in De Smet one last time in 1930. The De Smet *News* noted that the troupe was now playing in many of the smaller towns that they had seldom played in earlier. "The Robbins company has not been able to get their usual bookings in city theatres this year owing to the favor shown mechanical reproduction," the paper noted, "but their winter of playing has shown that the public is still glad to see the 'legitimate' production." But, in fact, this was the last hurrah for the company in De Smet, and by the 1930s traveling troupes stopped coming to town as the movies increasingly took over.[34]

Thanks to the railroad and the rapidly expanding communications media, which underwent a major transformation toward the end of the nineteenth century, De Smetites were able to participate in the popular culture that was permeating the entire country. From Shakespeare's *As You Like It*[35] to the absurdity of some of the song-and-dance companies, they were able to enjoy the same sorts of cultural wares that people from Boston to San Francisco were. The theater and vaudeville companies, opera singers, violinists, musical groups, minstrel shows, lecturers, stereopticon shows, and other entertainers and moral improvers introduced local people to what their contemporaries were experiencing and thinking elsewhere.

But activities in the opera house also invigorated and reinforced community ties by stimulating involvement by the town's residents themselves. The opera house became the site for high school activities, political rallies, and meetings and entertainments of every type. For a while in 1916 and 1917, wrestling matches featuring local men pitted against traveling "champions" were popular Saturday night entertainments there, but activities like this tended to come and go. Local talent performances were staged whenever someone had enough enthusiasm to organize them and find volunteers to do the necessary work. De Smet participated in a fad that took the region by storm in 1927 when it put on a "Womanless Wedding." For a fee, organizers came into little towns like De Smet and got the

A local talent play cast poses in the Couse Opera House. *(Courtesy South Dakota State Historical Society)*

menfolk to dress up in women's clothes for a spectacle that apparently stimulated great hilarity among both participants and audiences.[36]

By the late teens, most of these kinds of activities had moved out of the opera house and into other places. Sometime before the United States entered World War I in 1917, Edward H. Couse sold his business, and the hall became known as the Miller Opera House. Meanwhile, more and more activities were moving next door into the Floto Auditorium, whose owner, Fred Floto, also operated a pool hall and barber shop at the front of his building. Wrestling matches and Halloween parties were held in the Floto Hall as early as 1910, and by 1916 girls basketball games were being played there. Roller-skating, dances, and other activities also moved there during the late teens, and on some evenings movies were shown. The first movie in town had been shown at the Ely Building in 1910, but the first real movie theater was called the "Cozy." With the Floto advertising itself as a theater, there were two such places in town by 1916. In 1918 Floto sold out to William Klinkel, Sr., and his son George, and it became known as Klinkel Auditorium or Klinkel Hall. The operation remained in the Klinkel family until 1977. A young woman in town played piano for the silent movies that drew people in during the 1920s,[37] and people in town still remember Lawrence Welk playing there for dances, not once, but many times.

During the late twenties, as chain stores moved in force into small towns in South Dakota, the old Couse building housed a J. C. Penney's department store for about thirty years, after which Tom Ward of Bryant started a Variety (or "V") store there like the one he already operated in the town of Bryant, fifteen miles to the northeast. The Ward's Store, as it is called, is still run by the Ward family.[38]

Much changed during the decades that the opera house and the auditorium were in operation, but much remained the same, and Laura Ingalls Wilder's description of social entertainments and cultural events during the early 1880s overlaps considerably with the story gleaned from the historical record. Some of the places and kinds of activities just described played prominent roles in her narratives. The differences between her account and the full panoply of activity that existed in town derive from several circumstances. First, she was a teenager, not fully informed about or even interested in many things that went on. Second, she spent a lot of time on the family's homestead and so didn't have a chance to be part of many of the activities. Third, when she started getting romantically involved with Almanzo, some of their activities rotated around community events, but most of their time was spent roaming the countryside in Almanzo's buggy, and Laura's attention was probably focused on Almanzo. Finally, and most important, the narrative demands of storytelling forced Wilder to strip her account down to essentials and to include only the things that would keep the story moving briskly forward. After all, she was not writing social history, she was writing fiction.

In her first two novels set in and around De Smet, Wilder makes virtually no mention of community activities. *By the Shores of Silver Lake* briefly recounts early town building during the spring of 1880, and the socializing that is described occurs with the family's friends—the Boasts—and relatives. In *The Long Winter*, continual blizzards force people, especially women and children, to stay cooped up in their houses. Communal gathering places are the stores in town where the menfolk go to pass the time and catch up on news—Harthorne's grocery, Fuller's hardware, and Bradley's drugstore.[39]

Little Town on the Prairie, covering the period from the spring of 1881 to the end of 1882, describes some of the ways the townspeople improvised to entertain themselves during the second and third years of the town's existence, before traveling companies began to be very active and before the town had a good place to accommodate them. Pioneer settlers brought with them the tradition of "the glorious" Fourth of July, and Wilder described the event in De Smet in 1881, when Visscher V. Barnes, a young lawyer in town, gave her father some firecrackers to pass on to his girls. "Going in for politics," Pa explained to Laura and Carrie.[40]

With Christmas approaching, some townspeople organized a literary society to liven things up a bit. As Wilder told the story, it was a spontaneous decision by men sitting around the stove at Fuller's store, and when it was proposed they establish a permanent organization with elected officers, Pa insisted that they keep everything informal. Things may well have happened that way in 1881, but the literary societies that operated in town during 1883 and 1886 did have some organization to them and worked out weekly programs with schedule notices published in the paper. The first meeting, as described in *Little Town on the Prairie*, was an exciting spelling bee that Pa Ingalls won. One of the planned meetings was a debate on the relative merits of George Washington and Abraham Lincoln, with lawyer Barnes taking the side of the latter. Visscher V. Barnes, in fact, did become a well-known speaker on public issues. In a debate staged by the De Smet literary society in 1886, he joined Ven Owen and G. W. Elliot on the negative in a debate on the question, "Resolved: That the organization of the Knights of Labor is beneficial to the laboring classes and the country at large." Opposed to them on the affirmative side were J. F. Watson, John A. Owen, and J. B. Hall. Mrs. Bradley, wife of the druggist and a frequent participant in musical performances, sang such a sad song at one of the literaries, according to Wilder, that all of the women were weeping.[41]

The climax of the chapter entitled "The Whirl of Gaiety" was the spectacle of Mrs. Jarley's Wax Works in January 1882, in which several townspeople pretended to be wax figures depicting George Washington, Daniel Boone, Queen Elizabeth, and Sir Walter Raleigh. This is one of the few episodes in the novels for which an exact replica in real life can be determined, since in March 1885, a "Mrs. Jarley with her unique group of wax 'figgers' " was advertised to appear at the rink. The newspaper editor let his readers in on what they could expect: "These life-like representatives cannot be fitly described in a few words, but must be seen to be appreciated. We are desired by the management to say that all those who throughout the entertainment refrain from laughing will be presented the price of admission at the close of their good behavior."[42]

Were there actually two presentations of Mrs. Jarley's waxworks in De Smet, one in 1882, as retold by Wilder, and one in 1885, as reported in the newspaper? This appears unlikely, since surprise was the essence of the stunt. Instead, Wilder probably took an event that occurred later in a different setting and inserted it into her narrative of 1882. If she did, it would not be the only time she took scenes and events and reworked them in her narrative. A fuller picture of entertainments in town would require describing many more kinds of activities than those Wilder chose to include, but her literary instincts were good. She did not want to clutter her narrative with unimportant details.

Nevertheless, we should not too quickly assume that she rearranged everything to suit her art, because, for the most part, Wilder *did* rely upon her memory for the factual substratum of her narrative. A good example of this is Ben Woodworth's birthday party, upon which we can pin a specific date since his handwritten invitation survives (it is on display at the museum in Mansfield, Missouri). The invitation to supper on Saturday evening, January 28, reads almost exactly as it is reproduced in *Little Town on the Prairie*. Since January 28 occurred on a Saturday in 1882, we know the party occurred that year and that it fits into the narrative sequence as related in Wilder's novel.[43]

In the novels, Wilder reports that the last literary society meeting of the spring featured a local talent minstrel show. Then in the fall another round of social events began—church every Sunday, prayer meetings every Wednesday, two sociables planned by the Ladies' Aid, and talk of a Christmas tree. In November there was a week of revival meetings and then the school exhibition where Laura and Ida Brown exhibited their historical knowledge. By this time, Almanzo Wilder was "seeing her home," and in the last book of the series, *These Happy Golden Years*, the focus shifts from the public realm back to the private. Wilder describes her three teaching jobs, sleigh-riding parties, and buggy rides with Almanzo. Except for passing reference to a Christmas tree at the church and the sessions at the singing school, the events described in this book, covering January 1883 (just before her sixteenth birthday) to August 1885 (when she got married to Almanzo Wilder) are almost entirely private in nature.[44]

From a historical point of view, this private focus is unfortunate, since the surviving newspapers cover the record only from January 1883 on. We thus cannot match Wilder's narrative of the earlier period with the actual course of events as frozen in time by the newspaper editor in his local paragraphs. In addition, events described in the posthumously published *The First Four Years* all relate to Laura and Almanzo's struggles in trying to make an economic go of it on their farm north of town, not to social activities. If the couple ever got into town for church services or to attend any kind of social activities, we do not learn about them. If they knew anything about the grand opening of the Couse Opera House, we'll never know. They certainly had to come to town to buy supplies and to market their products, and we can presume that they did participate to some degree in the social life of the community. But in the absence of any evidence, we cannot know for sure.

Thus, we cannot be certain that Laura and Almanzo ever enjoyed any of the entertainments at the Couse Opera House after it was built, but we can presume that they must have entered it at least once or twice. For townspeople, more than farmers in the countryside, the opera house was a community center, bringing them together frequently to enjoy themselves, relieve their boredom, and link up, if only temporarily, with people in other communities along the railroad. The local opera house provided an important social cement, facilitating community cohesion in small towns. At the same time that it provided diversion from people's daily round of work and activity, it stimulated morale and local loyalty and, in so doing, contributed mightily to the quality of small-town life.

10 / Two Artists of the Prairie: Laura Ingalls Wilder and Harvey Dunn

Two of Wilder's novels contain the word "prairie" in their titles, and all of those set in and around De Smet provide detailed descriptions of the eastern Dakota prairie landscape. This is a transitional zone between the tallgrass prairie, which ranges toward the more humid east, and the shortgrass region that characterizes the more arid Great Plains to the west.[1] The look and the feel of the land strongly impressed the young Laura Ingalls, who took great delight in the wide open spaces and the freedom that they implied. Years later, when she wrote her novels, her descriptions sang with the joy, the beauty, and the pleasure of her surroundings. At the same time, she recognized that the prairie could also be menacing and grim.

For some who ventured out onto the prairie, such as the narrator of Willa Cather's *My Antonia*, there was nothing to see.[2] With few or no trees, waterways, hills, fences, or fields to focus their eyes on, many of the newly arrived settlers lacked the mental tools necessary to comprehend this seemingly faceless, empty environment. But for Laura, or at least the *remembered* Laura of *By the Shores of Silver Lake*, the prairie offered endless scenes of delight and wonder. In that novel Wilder recorded her impressions of the prairie as an adolescent traveling with her family in a wagon west from Tracy, Minnesota, on their way to the railroad camp near the future town of De Smet, their home for the winter. Spaciousness was the first image that struck her, but the newly settled farmsteads also lent the landscape an air of familiarity: "The whole sky was overhead and the prairie stretched away on all sides with farms scattered over it. The wagon went slowly, so there was time to see everything."[3]

At first Laura did not find much to describe aloud to her blind sister Mary as they wended their way across the prairie, for the brand new railroad grade seemed to extend endlessly toward the horizon and the fields and houses looked the same as they did back home, just newer and smaller. Nevertheless, there was something strange in the land they saw all about them, as Laura reconstructed the experience.

> But this was different from all the other times, not only because there was no cover on the wagon and no beds in it, but for some other reason. Laura couldn't say how, but this prairie was different.
>
> "Pa," she asked, "when you find the homestead, will it be like the one we had in Indian Territory?"
>
> Pa thought before he answered. "No," he said finally. "This is different country. I can't tell you how, exactly, but this prairie is different. It feels different."[4]

The prairie landscape, more than most other kinds, confounded simple efforts to comprehend it. Its very simplicity (at least *apparent* simplicity) seemed to guarantee that there would be opposite reactions among those who contemplated it—delight and wonder versus gloom and rejection; optimism and hope versus pessimism and defeat.[5] The primary impressions of the eastern Dakota prairie recorded by two other prominent authors, Ole Rolvaag and Hamlin Garland, were forbidding and dark.[6] But when it comes to visual art, the Dakota prairie is "Harvey Dunn country." His paintings portray an agricultural frontier that is full of sweat and hard work, danger and disappointment, frustrations and setbacks. Yet his pioneer settlers appear to triumph over the odds or at least persevere in the face of staggering difficulty, and the landscape in which this human drama takes place is rough but beautiful.[7]

Comparing Harvey Dunn's Dakota landscape paintings with Wilder's novelistic portrayals of the same area provides useful insights into the work of each of them. Juxtaposing their work seems like a natural thing to do, considering that the two grew up within a dozen miles of each other and were born only seventeen years apart. The kind of prairie frontier they depicted in their paintings and novels was of a piece—Wilder's books (the ones set around De Smet) covering the years from 1879 to 1889, and Dunn's paintings re-creating the life of homesteaders during the 1880s and 1890s.

The Ingalls family arrived by wagon in 1879, a few months before the Chicago and North Western track was laid across the prairie; the Dunn family located their land in 1880 and arrived to stay, by railroad emigrant car, the following year. Harvey Dunn, the second of three children (Caroline was a year older, Roy a year younger), was born in a twelve-foot by sixteen-foot homestead shanty on March 8, 1884, three miles south of Manchester, a railroad town eight miles down the track to the west of De Smet. Harvey Dunn grew big and strong as a youth, trailing oxen-drawn plows, harvesting wheat, and performing the dozens of tasks that filled the lives of every homestead family.

But in the nearby Esmond country school, which he attended for nine years, young Harvey filled the chalkboard with so many drawings, seeming never to tire of the activity, that his teacher felt compelled to hide the chalk so there would be enough left for the children's lessons. His father, a stern taskmaster, took no interest in Harvey's youthful artistry, considering it a frivolous diversion from the real business at hand—work. But his mother, Bersha, possessed some artistic talent of her own and encouraged her son's creativity, sitting beside him at the kitchen table and drawing along with him. It was her insistence that persuaded her husband to allow seventeen-year-old Harvey to trundle off to Brookings, fifty miles east along the railroad, where he signed up for classes in the preparatory school of South Dakota Agricultural College in the fall of 1901.

Like Laura Ingalls Wilder, whose Dakota prairie novels spanned her youth—from twelve to eighteen—Dunn's prairie paintings took their substance from his youthful memories before he went off to preparatory school. Reminiscing about his life in a letter to a college official at Brookings in 1941, Dunn observed that his interests had come full circle since he left the Redstone Creek on a path that took him beyond Brookings to the Chicago Art Institute and then to a stint as a student with the famous illustrator Howard Pyle at Wilmington, Delaware, before he finally took up residence in New Jersey. The result, he concluded, was that "my search of other horizons has led me around to my first."[8]

Wilder waited longer to turn her attention back to her Dakota horizon; she didn't begin her series of novels until she was in her early sixties, and she was almost seventy when she started working on the first one set in Dakota Territory. It was in 1930, just as she was beginning her work, that she and Dunn almost crossed paths. They had both been invited back to De Smet by newspaper editor Aubrey Sherwood for the town's annual Old Settlers' Day celebration on June 10 for the fiftieth anniversary of the town. Both accepted the invitation, but only Dunn actually made it to South Dakota that year; Wilder was forced to cancel at the last moment and stayed at home. But both sent poems to editor Sherwood, who printed them several weeks later in a weekly edition of the De Smet *News*.[9]

The Wilders did return to De Smet for the celebration the following year, but Laura never had a chance to meet the artist. In 1938 her daughter Rose ran into Dunn at a meeting of the South Dakota Society in New York City. They were introduced to each other by Aubrey Sherwood's brother Vincent, who worked for a New York City music company.[10] Wilder was well-acquainted with Dunn's work, which had appeared regularly since 1906 in national magazines such as *Harper's, Colliers, Scribner's, Century,*

McCalls, and especially the *Saturday Evening Post*. More-
over, she was related to him by marriage. In 1901 her sister
Grace had married Nate Dow, a brother of Dunn's mother.
Until Grace's death in 1941, the childless couple lived on
several farms around Manchester, in the town itself, and
for a time in De Smet with Ma and Mary. Through Grace,
Ma and Mary kept Laura informed about Dunn's budding
magazine illustration career.[11]

Today, we might wonder why Dunn was never called
upon to illustrate Lane's Dakota frontier stories when
they were top-billed in the *Saturday Evening Post* during
the 1930s. Born just two years before her on a prairie homestead only about a dozen miles from Laura and Almanzo's
place, Dunn would have been eminently qualified to do
the artwork for her *Let the Hurricane Roar*, serialized in
the *Post* in October 1932 and published in book form the
following year, and *Free Land*, serialized in the *Post* in
March and April 1938 and published in book form in May.
Instead, one of Dunn's students, W. H. D. Koerner, was
chosen to illustrate the first book. Another Dunn protégé,
Grant Reynard, also provided illustrations for some of
Lane's work. If Wilder had begun her series of novels with
one set in Dakota, Dunn would have been a perfect choice
as illustrator. But *Little House in the Big Woods*, published in 1932, was set in Wisconsin, and when the Da-
kota-based novels came out in the late thirties and early
forties, Harper and Row stayed with the same illustrator.

Sometime during the 1950s, Wilder told Aubrey Sherwood: "Harvey Dunn has done a great thing in his paintings and it does seem as though they and my stories
should be connected in some way. I should be proud to
have our names connected because of our work."[12] The
De Smet editor took great pride in the role he played in
promoting the art of Dunn and Wilder in South Dakota.
In 1950, when the editor and his wife were visiting Dunn
in Tenafly, Sherwood commented, "I wish the folks back
home could see what we are seeing." Dunn, who was suffering from cancer at the time (he died two years later), responded enthusiastically to Sherwoood's chance remark.

He quickly arranged to bring out forty-two of his works for display in the De Smet Masonic Lodge Hall during the summer of 1950. Sherwood later prodded South Dakota State College president Fred Leinbach to drive over to De Smet to view the paintings, and afterward the college executive offered a permanent home for them in Brookings. The college then built an art center to house the collection. Although Dunn's national reputation as a magazine illustrator was already secure, he yearned to achieve lasting impact from the prairie paintings he worked on from the mid-twenties until his death. Without Sherwood's intervention, that collection may well have been scattered, and the achievement it represented may never have been fully recognized.[13]

A publicity campaign was not required to establish Laura Ingalls Wilder's fame, but Sherwood's efforts did remind South Dakotans of her singular contribution to frontier history, especially to Dakota history. His invitation to attend the 1938 Old Settlers' Day celebration arrived at a particularly opportune time for Wilder, because she was working on her first novel set in Dakota at the time. The trip that she and Almanzo made back to De Smet gave her a chance to talk to old friends and to check facts and stories for use in the rest of the novels she was planning to write about De Smet. This trip to De Smet was her third since moving to Missouri in 1894. She had come home when her father died in 1902 and then had returned for Old Settlers' Day in 1931.[14] Her final trip to South Dakota would come in 1939, when she and Almanzo visited Grace and Nate in Manchester for the last time, then went on to see her sister Carrie Swanzey in Keystone in the Black Hills before driving to Colorado and back home to Mansfield.[15]

By 1938 and 1939 the Dakota prairie was greening up again as rainfall levels were returning to normal after almost a decade of severe drought. Old memories would have stirred in Laura and Almanzo as they drove along Highway 14 next to the tracks of the Chicago and North Western Railroad, the same route that had originally brought them to the Dakota frontier sixty years earlier. Many of the original buildings were still standing, although many new, more modern structures had sprouted alongside them. The highway, too, was modern, paved just a couple of years earlier. Fences, telephone poles, silos, windmills, and other signs of modern civilization dotted and cut across the prairie, framing it and modifying it. Had they been in a plane instead of a car, they could have perceived more distinctly the endless checkerboard pattern the federal rectangular surveys had imposed upon the land.

But when the Ingalls and Dunn families first arrived in Dakota Territory in 1879 and 1880, all of that lay in the distant future. The Dakota Indians and their sustenance, the buffalo, had been only recently killed off or chased from the scene; in fact, a few Indians continued to roam the territory for several years. The tallgrass prairie stood waist-high, high enough for little girls like Laura and Carrie to get lost in.[16] Human hands soon shaped and modified the landscape, but for a while, at least, nature held sway over humans in determining the look of the land.[17]

It was this relatively pristine landscape that Wilder and Dunn later portrayed in their respective ways. Both depicted an idealized landscape, impressive in dimension and bathed in color. The enormity of the prairie—its seemingly limitless dimensions—stands out prominently in the work of both. "This prairie is like an enormous meadow, stretching out in every direction, to the very edge of the world," Laura told Mary. Although she could not describe this new place adequately in words, Laura immediately sensed its effect on the settlers. It rearranged people's perceptions. The further west they traveled, the smaller they all seemed. Even time seemed to be different here. The further west they went, the less they seemed to be getting anywhere. Sight, sound, and other senses seemed to converge. Space was enormous, but there was also an "enormous stillness"—an "enormous silence"—that seemed to envelop everything.[18]

Like many other western artists, Wilder tended to exag-

Something for Supper, by Harvey Dunn. *(Courtesy South Dakota Art Museum Collection, Brookings, South Dakota)*

gerate space and distance when she described the Dakota prairie.[19] Besides being "enormous," it was characterized in *By the Shores of Silver Lake* as "huge," "vast," and "immense."[20] But as Laura matured in the later books, the prairie began to take on a more human shape, losing some of its enormity. Always there was the wind, the sky, and the sun or the clouds that might hide its vastness. The emptiness of the prairie, save for the undulating grasses, was broken only by a lone cottonwood or a homesteader's shanty here and there. All over the prairie wildflowers bloomed, punctuating the green grass with iridescent shades of yellow and blue, pink and lavender.[21]

The prairie, then, was beautiful to Laura. It was her delight. More than that, it was meaningful, especially in conveying a sense of freedom and playfulness. But its meaning did not remain constant, rather it shifted with conditions and the seasons. In winter, when the snow covered everything and the wind howled, the prairie was desolate and cold in contrast to her snug, cozy house. But when the sun came out, the cold could transform the glittering, icy world into a glorious day. When the prairie grass was covered with snow, there was no trace of a road or a path, no sign that anyone or anything had been there. This "trackless sea" was confusing and frightening to eyes looking for landmarks. Colors on the prairie during winter were soft, muted—pale browns, faint greens and purples, fawn-gray and gray-blue.[22]

Come spring, life sprang up anew on the prairie. Angleworms slithered out of the ground, gophers worked to get at the corn, wild ducks and geese pierced the sky.[23] The prairie was alive. It was beautiful, but it could also threaten. Blackbirds and pests invaded the grain and Spanish needles contested for growing space with the hay. Laura observed: "The prairie looks so beautiful and gentle. But I wonder what it will do next. Seems like we have to fight it all the time."[24]

People's perceptions of the prairie, therefore, varied according to conditions, their own predispositions, and the purposes with which they viewed it. The prairie was a place in which to work, to hunt, to pick wildflowers, to take buggy rides, to gaze at sunsets, to battle the elements. For the adolescent Wilder, it was primarily a landscape to observe, in the way that a tourist might. But in her final, posthumously published book about her first four years of married life with Almanzo, what had been true only in a small way earlier now became the dominant theme: the two faces of the prairie—the prairie as source of sustenance and survival and the prairie as threat to their well-being. No longer dependent on her parents for food and shelter, Laura and her husband had to ensure their own living from the soil. Unfortunately, they picked a poor time to begin farming, as wet seasons gave way to dry ones during the late 1880s. The drought and a variety of other scourges finally drove them out.

Laura still "liked the horses and enjoyed the freedom and spaciousness of the wide prairie land, with the wind forever waving the tall wild grass in the sloughs and rustling through the short curly buffalo grass, so green on the upland swells in spring and so silvery-gray and brown in summer."[25] But in *The First Four Years*, Wilder seldom refers to the beauties of the prairie. The spectator point of view gives way to a participatory vantage point in which the arithmetic of farming defines success. Laura cooks for threshers in the fall and Almanzo buys a new breaking plow for $55, paying half cash and borrowing the rest. A harrow to work the land, a new McCormick binder that cost $200, a hayrake, and a mowing machine also had to be paid for and maintained.[26] At this stage, the prairie had become a resource that required substantial borrowed capital to exploit. It was a recalcitrant resource, too, giving up its largesse reluctantly and conspiring with locusts, hailstorms, and drought to ruin a young farm couple.

It is this primordial struggle between the farm family and the elements that Harvey Dunn portrayed so memorably in his prairie paintings. Many an episode described in Wilder's novels finds its counterpart in Dunn's dramatic renderings of frontier life. Good examples are three winter scenes—*After the Blizzard, School Day's End,* and *30 Degrees below Zero*—showing deeply piled snow that is packed so hard people can walk on it, so high that it almost buries schoolhouses and homesteaders' shanties and envelops animals in its whirling fury. Pictorially, these paintings evoke the same thoughts and feelings as Wilder's dramatic descriptions of blizzards in *The Long Winter.*

The subject of *A Driver of Oxen*—a square-jawed, squint-eyed, wiry, and determined frontiersman—typified the motivated, hard-working, and gritty men that Dunn painted to evoke the spirit of the people who settled the prairie. This figure could easily have been Charles Ingalls leading his family across the prairie or driving his oxen into town. Many people living around Manchester and De Smet thought they knew who the painter's models were for pictures like these and tried to identify the places he used as backdrops for his scenes. But Dunn's purpose was not to portray specific individuals, places, or events, but to recapture the moment of settlement, the mood of the settlers, the look of the landscape, the feel of the time.[27]

Although realistic in approach, Dunn's prairie paintings resemble, to some degree, impressionistic works in their vagueness and in their use of color. To truly apprehend and appreciate many of them, it is necessary to step back twenty or thirty feet from the canvas and view them from a distance. Dunn's purpose was to capture a mood, to re-create the spirit of homesteading, and in this effort he was spectacularly successful. "Paint a little less of the facts, and a little more of the *spirit*," he liked to tell students in his classroom. "Paint more with feeling than with thought."[28] Imagination and empathy, he believed, were the crucial ingredients of any successful art. One had to *become* the person one was painting. The artist was not out to capture surface reality, but *inner* reality, which required more than mere seeing. Dunn preached to all who would listen: "Imagination is just about the most perfect thing there is. The way we can visualize a picture in our imagination is about as close to perfection as we'll ever know."[29]

Dunn practiced his own advice—to search for the epic, to "paint importantly." His approach was poetical and musical.[30] In urging his students to make their work sing, Dunn resembled Wilder, for whom music was also of central importance. The songs she sang, many of which she reproduced in her books, helped infuse her life with meaning and structure. She would have understood and agreed with Dunn's observation, "If you're going to make an illustration you must take poetry and song into it."[31]

For the last quarter-century of his life—from around 1927, when he took a western tour with his son Robert and his artist friend Arthur Mitchell, until his death in 1952—Harvey Dunn returned almost annually to his ancestral haunts to sketch and visit with friends and relatives and relive his boyhood days. He stayed with his sister Carrie on her farmstead several miles south of Manchester and drove into town to banter with people at the local cafe or over at Wallums Corner, a filling station a half mile east of town where the country road to Carrie's place intersected Highway 14. Manchester's population of several dozen people was not even listed in the census then because the town was unincorporated. But Dunn, the eastern sophisticate and successful magazine illustrator who lived in tasteful affluence back in New Jersey, mingled easily and unaffectedly with these people—his kind of people—for he had come from them. His wife, Tulla, once came out with him to Manchester and found it dull and retrograde; the homefolks, for their part, considered her haughty and distant. She never came back, usually scheduling a European tour while her husband went "back home" during the summertime.[32]

Except for a portrait and a landscape or two, Dunn never painted in South Dakota. Rather, he filled his sketchbooks with blue and brown crayon and took them back to his Tenafly studio to rework into finished paintings. He always advised his students to let their picture express an idea. Simply to paint what they saw was a waste of time. "Let it be an expression rather than a description," he told them.[33] That is why he insisted on painting in the studio. Artists should go as far as they could in rendering their expression, Dunn believed. Then if they needed to remind themselves of how a tree or an object looked, they could go out into the field, sketch it in pencil, and bring it back into the studio to paint it in.[34]

The ideas Dunn sought to embody in his prairie paintings coincided with themes that Wilder pursued in her novels: the challenge of weather and the elements, the immensity of space on the prairie, the arrival of settlers, the grit and determination of both women and men in eking out survival, the physical burden of work, the beauty of the prairie landscape, and the importance of education and religion in people's lives. Both focused on a similar moment in history—the first few years of settlement on the prairie. Wilder's goal was more mundane: to tell stories she had heard and experienced in as simple and direct a way as possible. In the process, she transformed the concrete into the universal. Dunn's purpose was universal from the start, not to portray particular people and places in time, but to re-create out of his own experience and observation the general frontier environment and, in the process, to say something significant about humanity.

Dunn told stories with his paintings just as Wilder painted pictures with her stories. The difference between them was that the latter could give much fuller expression to the details of prairie life in her novels than Dunn could with line and color in his paintings. Always Dunn sought drama, though his was not the drama of actual historical events. About the only rendition of an identifiable person in Dunn's prairie paintings is his *Jedediah Smith in the Badlands*, a portrait of the famous mountain man who is reputed to have been the first white man to visit the Dakota Badlands during the early 1800s.

The drama that Dunn sought to capture lay mainly in the mundane goings-on of everyday life, not in specific events or heroic individuals. "Look for the dramatic presentation even if you're painting a flower," he told his students. "Everything is dramatic if we can only see it so."[35] Like his mentor Howard Pyle, Dunn preached service "to the majesty of simple things."[36] Dunn's ability to achieve this goal helps explain the great popularity of his paintings among South Dakotans and others who, like Dunn, appreciate the virtues of simple living. He was unexcelled as a magazine illustrator during the decade before 1917 and was selected by the U.S. Army as one of eight official artists to travel with the troops during World War I. He was a teacher of John Steuart Curry, and he was widely revered by the students who took his art courses in Leonia and Tenafly, New Jersey, and at the Grand Central School of Art in New York City. Many of them went on to achieve recognition and fame in their own right. Nevertheless, Dunn, the prairie painter of the thirties and forties, never received the acclaim that his fellow regionalists—Curry, Grant Wood, and Thomas Hart Benton—achieved. While the paintings of those three artists were establishing reputations for their creators, Dunn had decided to keep most of his works in his studio in New Jersey until he deeded them to South Dakota State College in 1950. This decision may account for his relative obscurity. In recent years, however, Dunn's prairie paintings have demonstrated their popularity and resonance with the public by being chosen over and over again as illustrations for American history textbooks and other publications.

The current public popularity of Dunn's paintings is undeniable. The explanation for it parallels the reasons for the popularity of Wilder's novels. Countless homes in South Dakota have framed prints of Harvey Dunn's paintings hanging on their walls, just as many homes have boxed sets or individual copies of Wilder's novels on their bookshelves. Schools and public buildings, likewise, are festooned with Dunn prints, and the Wilder books have been read to classrooms of elementary students for decades. Both the paintings and the novels depict a heroic stage of American history—the last agricultural frontier of the late 1800s, on which families courageously confronted difficult obstacles and overcame them through determination, hard work, and strength of character. Both artists took a realistic approach to their subjects, portraying them in a straightforward, easy to understand fashion. Both implied that hard work and strength of character will earn their just reward, although the outcome is never certain and the challenges seem never-ending. Both emphasized people and seldom let the environment push them out of the forefront. Dunn seldom painted landscapes with no people present, and even when his human figures look tiny on an immense landscape, they seem to convey a sense of perseverance and indomitability that will win out in the end. "No scene or landscape is of any importance except as a background for human endeavor," he said.[37]

Part of the popularity of Dunn's paintings and Wilder's novels derives from their participation in broader cultural and artistic trends. Both partook of the romantic tradition of western art.[38] In combining prosaic elements with romantic ones, they drew upon myths and symbols that have transformed our vision of the West from a merely descriptive one to an imaginatively romantic one. In Wilder's recounting of her family's trek to Dakota Territory in

By the Shores of Silver Lake and in Dunn's rendition of arriving settlers in *Something for Supper* and *In Search of the Land of Milk and Honey*, we find classic examples of one variety of the romantic vision—the pastoral, elegiac version promoted by artists from George Catlin and Karl Bodmer to Thomas Moran and Albert Bierstadt. Most striking, the image of the "prairie madonna," whose artistic precursors can be traced back to medieval Europe, is invoked by the pioneer women who figure so prominently in Dunn's work and by Ma Ingalls in Wilder's books. But Dunn's prairie madonna differs from the memorable counterpart created by one of his students, W. H. D. Koerner, whose strikingly beautiful and fragile homesteader hardly seems capable of the kind of strenuous and endless labor that Dunn's *Pioneer Woman* and other portrayals suggest. Picturing the prairie as a garden was another way of romanticizing it. and Dunn helped promote this tradition, especially with works like his best-known painting, *The Prairie Is My Garden*.[39]

Dunn and Wilder both benefited from the high regard with which the frontier period of American history is held by the general public. Frederick Jackson Turner's famous frontier thesis considered the margin between "civilization and savagery" to be the breeding ground for specifically American traits, such as democracy, freedom, and equality. The pioneers, in his interpretation, were resilient, adaptable, creative, and progressive, and Dunn's and Wilder's homesteaders, either explicitly or implicitly, fit that description.[40]

Dunn and Wilder also worked simultaneously with the regionalist painters of the 1930s and drew upon the same resources that inspired them.[41] Many factors were operating to legitimize and popularize regional themes and rural values during the Depression decade. The vogue for documentary sanctioned realistic portrayals of prairie life like those of Dunn and Wilder.[42] Thomas Hart Benton was especially successful in demonstrating how the depiction of ordinary life could intersect with American myths and dreams, and Wilder's and Dunn's work likewise gained prominence through their artful combination of simple descriptions of everyday life and grander themes that can only be called mythic.[43]

But showing how Wilder's and Dunn's works fit into the broader artistic framework of the age can only go so far in explaining their enduring popularity. Ultimately, their popular acclaim depends on the particular moment the two artists chose to focus their attention upon—the first few years of settlement on the Dakota prairie, when life was simpler and more innocent than it would be later. (Wilder's earlier books depicting the Wisconsin, Kansas, and Minnesota frontiers also avoided social conflict and controversy, since they were written from the vantage point of a preteen who largely failed to perceive the kinds of evils and contradictions that would become more apparent as she matured.)

This point becomes clearer when we consider what Wilder and Dunn left out of their depictions. Politics, first of all. The Farmers' Alliance emerged in Dakota Territory in 1885 and, following in its wake, agrarian protestors in 1890 established an independent party, a predecessor of the soon-to-be-formed Populist party.[44] Although we can learn something about the "arithmetic of farming" and the burdens of drought, grasshoppers, debt, and inadequate farm prices in Wilder's novels, these problems are never translated into political terms. And the closest we get to a depiction of the historical grievances of the farmer in Dunn is a couple of paintings depicting drought conditions—*Dust* and *A Few Drops of Rain* (which could have been referring to the 1930s as well as to the 1880s or 1890s). Generally, the hardships of farmers as they are depicted in the works of Dunn and Wilder are not rooted in the political conflicts of the time but are portrayed as timeless struggles between people and the land and the elements, with little doubt left in the viewer's and reader's mind about who would ultimately prevail.

Wilder's narrative description of building railroads, homesteading, planting crops, purchasing machinery, borrowing money, and struggling steadfastly against the elements subsumes many of the story elements that were described over and over again by early pioneer settlers. Although acknowledging that exploitation sometimes occurred (Daniel Loftus's effort to profit from the townspeople during the hard winter of 1880-1881), admitting that some people succumbed to fear and madness (Mrs. Brewster's nocturnal knife wielding when Laura taught at the Brewster school), and agreeing that family relationships could be cruel and inconsiderate (in the family she stayed with while she sewed shirts in town),[45] Wilder's focus was primarily upon the positive aspects of frontier community life, emphasizing mutual support and caring and depicting triumph over adversity. By the time she fell in love with Almanzo Wilder, Laura's whole outlook on life was permeated by stargazing wonder and expectation.

Dunn's paintings went even further in stripping his subject matter of negative references. Like Wilder, he placed individuals and families in the center of his vision and sought to draw out the qualities that made up their character. Seldom are groups of more than two or three people depicted in his paintings; almost always it is an individual or a family group that holds center stage. Thus, the kinds of communal activities that get so much attention in Wilder's novels—religious revival services, Fourth of July celebrations, horse races, school games, literary society meetings, birthday parties, and sociables—do not show up in Dunn's prairie paintings. The closest we get to a community ritual or activity is the prairie funeral pictured in *I Am the Resurrection and the Life. After School,* one of Dunn's most widely reproduced paintings, and *School Day's End* each depict six or seven children heading home at the end of the school day, but they are going in different directions and not interacting as a group.

The primary theme of the prairie paintings is the way in which individuals and families made a living and made a way of life—their efforts, struggles, expectations, perseverance, and continuity on the land. The kinds of qualities admired by South Dakotans and their fellow prairie dwellers show up here in abundance—a solid work ethic, optimism, individualism, determination, and contentment. Absent political conflict, absent ethnic divisions, absent debate over social and cultural values, it's no wonder these simple, self-reliant, hard-working pioneers appear so heroic, so admirable.

South Dakotans liked what they saw in Dunn's pictures and identified with the people he portrayed. His homesteaders seemed to epitomize the character of the state. "What is it that makes Harvey Dunn important to his native state?" inquired the editor of the *State College Farmer and Home Maker* in its premier issue in 1953. Referring to a Dunn painting on the cover of the issue and another one at the head of the column, he answered his own question, "They portray the life of the early pioneer in this state—the essential spirit of the state itself." The editor went on to quote former State College president Fred Leinbach's grateful response to Dunn's "truly marvelous" gift to the school, "In his paintings he has caught the enthusiasm, the determination and the undaunted spirit of the pioneer characteristics which have given a great heritage to South Dakota's people." The Northwestern Public Service Company, which had chosen Dunn's paintings for the covers of thirteen consecutive annual reports, expressed its admiration for the artist in its 1977 report, which featured Dunn's *Old Settlers*: "His paintings reflect realistically the heritage of the prairies he knew and loved so well. *Old Settlers* portrays the determined character of the men and women who met the challenges of early-day farming and ranching in the Midwest."[46]

Strangely enough, significantly enough, Dunn's prairie paintings are devoid of railroads and advanced farm machinery and technology, despite their central importance in the settlers' lives. The railroad brought the Dunns to Manchester in the first place and was responsible for transporting their grain and livestock products to market and bringing in the consumer items they purchased at stores in town. Most homesteaders went into debt to purchase all kinds of machinery from harvesters and binders to threshing machines and sulky plows.[47] Yet the only kinds of farm implements present in Dunn's prairie paintings are simple plows, wagons, and stoneboats (to haul away rocks and stones).

Dunn, who worked in the fields around Manchester until he went off to preparatory school at Brookings in 1901, surely must have had some experience with more sophisticated farm machinery and may have worked with threshing crews on farms around the area during the fall harvest season. In a cover illustration for *The American Legion Magazine* in October 1932, he shows a farm worker pitching bundles while big threshing machines work in the background, and in *Woman at the Pump*, there are the vague outlines of what might be a tractor and a grain reaper of some sort in the background. But for the most part even a hint of sophisticated technology is absent from his work. His quintessential frontier farmer is the plowman pictured in *Buffalo Bones Are Plowed Under*. Even the cover illustration of a farmer he did for the August 1943 issue of *The American Legion Magazine* shows a rustic scene with a horse-drawn haymow in the background, even though the war crisis was rapidly mechanizing American agriculture.

Also puzzling is the fact that Dunn almost entirely ignored small towns in his prairie painting phase. His gaze, almost without exception, was directed toward the rural countryside. Apparently the only South Dakota town scene he did in oil was the January 1934 cover for *The American Legion Monthly* entitled *The Return to the Prairie Home*. According to his friend Aubrey Sherwood, Dunn took special interest in the painting, as it was meant to depict Manchester. (It was one of his few paintings intended to represent a particular location.) Sherwood thought he could recognize the town's bank in the left background of the painting and a long, low building on the right. But besides a sketch of Manchester's main street published in *American Artist* in June 1942 and a couple of other sketches of the town that remain in private collections, Dunn's work does not deal with towns in any way.[48]

Why not? Dunn was seventeen when he left South Dakota and would have remembered his trips to Manchester and possibly other towns in the area. But he apparently was unwilling to trust to his memory to re-create the look of the late-nineteenth-century town. He felt comfortable painting rural scenes, because the people and the landscape had not changed that much and many of the old houses, barns, and other buildings were still standing. Combining imagination and observation, he could re-create the look of farmers plowing, women cutting flowers, and children walking home from school. But just as he avoided picturing farm machinery any more sophisticated than simple plows, he also shied away from painting town scenes. Thus, his prairie scenes concentrate on a thin slice of time, the first several years of settlement before the new machines became prevalent.

In sum, Dunn's prairie paintings do a wonderful job of evoking the mood of a particular moment in the history of the frontier, capturing the spirit and character of pioneers energetically working to establish themselves on the land. But the period he depicts was short-lived. Soon industrial forces would transform that landscape and that society. In the imagery of Leo Marx, "the machine invaded the garden," thus complicating social relationships and social progress.[49] Perhaps it is unfair to describe either Dunn's or Wilder's artistic re-creation of life on the late-nineteenth-century Dakota frontier as "nostalgic." But Dunn himself invited use of the term "sentimental" to describe how he reacted to scenes from his prairie upbringing. He did not shy away from sentiment. "What is sentimental?" he asked students in his art classes. "I suppose what appeals to the sentiments. But are we interested in anything that *doesn't* appeal to the sentiments? I think bankers and people who deal with hard facts would get a lot more out of life if they'd get away from the 'brick and mortar' and *be* sentimental once in a while."[50]

But Dunn's sentimentality did not negate his realism. The tension that existed between the two in his art helps explain the difference between his depiction of two old ru-

Old Settlers, by Harvey Dunn. *(Courtesy South Dakota Art Museum Collection, Brookings, South Dakota)*

ral farm people and the much more famous rendition of a similar subject by his regionalist counterpart Grant Wood. The Iowan's *American Gothic* is a stylized, self-conscious, and ironic portrait of a man and a woman that almost invites a sarcastic and condescending reaction. Few viewers can find heroic qualities in the couple. Dunn's *Old Settlers,* painted a decade later, might conceivably be open to an ironic interpretation, but the expressions on the faces of his wizened and stoic subjects and the more realistic background they are set against prompt the observer to take these characters at face value and to try to understand who they are and why they are there.

Dunn's intent in portraying the people he painted was not to view them in a clinical and detached fashion, not to treat them ironically or sarcastically, not to glorify them or debase them. Rather, it was to take them on their own terms, to try to understand them, and, without glorifying them, to celebrate them and the human spirit that made them persist on the land. These same impulses motivated Laura Ingalls Wilder in her writings. The resulting works of art have garnered for both Wilder and Dunn the continuing admiration and respect of their readers and viewers.

What ultimately connects Dunn and Wilder is a common attitude toward life. Both lived life deeply, drinking in its beauty and fullness; each sought to make life for other people more joyous and meaningful. "Paint with light, not darkness—with love, not hate," Dunn exhorted his students.[51] "Paint the charm, the warmth, the beauty and the abundance of the day and of the people," he advised.[52] He also liked to repeat Robert Henri's observation that "a man's art is the expression of the joy he takes in living."[53] In all of this, he was expressing, in the words of Dean Cornwell, "a basic American philosophy."[54] That philosophy, in its verve, joy, optimism, and positive attitude, was totally in keeping with Laura Ingalls Wilder's own.

As she wrote in an article for a rural newspaper in 1917 at the time of the Russion revolution: "I believe we would be happier to have a personal revolution in our individual lives and go back to simpler living and more direct thinking. It is the simple things of life that make living worth while, the sweet fundamental things such as love and duty, work and rest and living close to nature. There are no hothouse blossoms that can compare in beauty and fragrance to my bouquet of wild flowers."[55]

Notes

The following abbreviations will be used throughout the Notes:

LIW	Laura Ingalls Wilder
RWL	Rose Wilder Lane
Wilder Papers	Laura Ingalls Wilder Papers, State Historical Society of Missouri, Columbia, Missouri
Lane Papers	Rose Wilder Lane Papers, Herbert Hoover Presidential Library, West Branch, Iowa

Wilder's original autobiography, "Pioneer Girl," written in 1930, exists in three different versions—her original handwritten draft and two edited versions that were sent to agents Carl Brandt and George Bye. Since all of these versions are cited in the Notes, a shortened citation has been used. Where the information referred to is contained in the final version (the one sent to Bye), that draft is cited. When the information is in the Brandt but not the Bye version, that draft is cited. Where the information is contained in the original handwritten manuscript but was excised from the typewritten drafts sent to Brandt and Bye, Wilder's original is, of course, cited. The following short forms of citation are employed:

LIW, "Pioneer Girl" draft—Wilder's handwritten draft, Wilder Papers, State Historical Society of Missouri (microfilm).
LIW, "Pioneer Girl" (Brandt version)—version sent to Carl Brandt, Lane Papers, Hoover Presidential Library.
LIW, "Pioneer Girl" (Bye version)—version sent to George Bye, Lane Papers, Hoover Presidential Library.

Wilder's handwritten drafts of her eight novels (sometimes in two different forms) are located in the following places:

State Historical Society of Missouri (microfilm; originals located at Wilder Memorial Association, Mansfield, Missouri):
By the Shores of Silver Lake
Farmer Boy
Little House in the Big Woods
Little House on the Prairie
On the Banks of Plum Creek
Detroit Public Library, Rare Book Room:
The Long Winter
These Happy Golden Years
Pomona, California, Public Library:
Little Town on the Prairie

All of the books were published in New York by Harper and Row. Publication dates for the books were:
Little House in the Big Woods, 1932
Farmer Boy, 1933
Little House on the Prairie, 1935
On the Banks of Plum Creek, 1937
By the Shores of Silver Lake, 1939
The Long Winter, 1940
Little Town on the Prairie, 1941
These Happy Golden Years, 1943
The First Four Years, 1971

Chapter 1. Introduction

1. Russel B. Nye, "History and Literature: Branches of the Same Tree," in *Essays on History and Literature*, ed. Robert H. Bremner (Columbus: Ohio State University Press, 1966), p. 159.

2. René Wellek, "Destroying Literary Studies," *New Criterion* 2 (December 1983): 7.

3. LIW and RWL, *A Little House Sampler*, ed. William T. Anderson (Lincoln: University of Nebraska Press, 1988), p. 217.

4. Lionel Trilling, *The Liberal Imagination: Essays on Literature and Society* (New York: Viking, 1951), pp. 211–12.

5. LIW, "Pioneer Girl" (Bye version), pp. 9–10, 60–63.

6. LIW, *Little Town on the Prairie* draft, pp. 28–30, Pomona, Calif., Public Library; LIW, *Little Town on the Prairie* (New York: Harper & Row, 1941), chap. 8.; William Holtz, *The Ghost in the Little House: A Life of Rose Wilder Lane* (Columbia: University of Missouri Press, 1993), pp. 306–7.

7. Rosa Ann Moore was the first to document extensively the

close collaboration between mother and daughter in the writing of the novels and the extent to which artistic considerations shaped the raw materials (see "Laura Ingalls Wilder's Orange Notebooks and the Art of the Little House Books," *Children's Literature* 4 [1975]: 105-19; "The Little House Books: Rose-Colored Classics," ibid. 7 [1978]: 7-16; "Laura Ingalls Wilder and Rose Wilder Lane: The Chemistry of Collaboration," *Children's Literature in Education* 11 [Autumn 1980]: 101-9). William T. Anderson went further in demonstrating the guiding influence of the daughter, especially during the early years of their collaboration, but he also emphasizes that the novels were rooted in historical experience (see "The Literary Apprenticeship of Laura Ingalls Wilder," *South Dakota History* 13 [Winter 1983]: 285-331, and "Laura Ingalls Wilder and Rose Wilder Lane: The Continuing Collaboration," ibid. 16 [Summer 1986]: 89-143; see also Janet Spaeth, *Laura Ingalls Wilder* [Boston: Twayne, 1987], pp. 1, 34, 86, 93-95). Holtz, in *The Ghost in the Little House*, has gone further than anyone previously to document the heavy indebtedness of mother to daughter in the writing of the books.

Chapter 2. Place and Community in Wilder's De Smet

1. LIW, *By the Shores of Silver Lake* (New York: Harper and Row, 1939), p. 254.

2. Robert V. Hine, *Community on the American Frontier: Separate but Not Alone* (Norman: University of Oklahoma Press, 1980), p. 247.

3. LIW, *These Happy Golden Years* (New York: Harper and Row, 1943), p. 37.

4. De Smet *Leader*, May 5 and September 22, 1883. On publishers of bird's-eye views, see Seymour I. Schwartz and Ralph E. Ehrenberg, *The Mapping of America* (New York: Harry N. Abrams, 1980), pp. 298-99, and Walter W. Ristow, *American Maps and Mapmakers: Commercial Cartography in the Nineteenth Century* (Detroit: Wayne State University Press, 1985), pp. 261-63. For a discussion of South Dakota views, see "Artists Draw South Dakota: Panoramic Views of Pioneer Towns," *South Dakota History* 8 (Summer 1978): 221-49.

5. De Smet *Leader*, April 28, 1883.

6. Ibid., May 5, 1883.

7. Ibid., March 10, 24, April 7, 14, October 20, 1883. See also John N. Vogel, *Great Lakes Lumber on the Great Plains: The*

Laird, *Norton Lumber Company in South Dakota* (Iowa City: University of Iowa Press, 1992), esp. chaps. 5–6.

8. According to James F. Hamburg, *The Influence of Railroads upon the Processes and Patterns of Settlement in South Dakota* (New York: Arno Press, 1981), 227 of the 285 towns platted between 1878 and 1889 in the area that later became South Dakota were railroad towns (p. 90). See also Kenneth Hammer, "Dakota Railroads" (Ph.D. dissertation, South Dakota State University, 1966), pp. 183–201, and Robert J. Casey and W. A. S. Douglas, *Pioneer Railroad: The Story of the Chicago and North Western System* (New York: Whittlesey House, 1948), pp. 134–39, 159–71.

9. Sam B. Warner, Jr., in *Streetcar Suburbs: The Process of Growth in Boston, 1870–1900* (Cambridge, Mass.: Harvard University Press, 1962), makes a similar point about a city built on a large scale. "The Boston metropolis is the product of hundreds of thousands of separate decisions," he writes. "It was a partnership between large institutions and individual investors and homeowners" (pp. 3–4).

10. John Brinckerhoff Jackson, *Discovering the Vernacular Landscape* (New Haven, Conn.: Yale Univeresity Press, 1984), p. 12.

11. On T-towns, see John C. Hudson, *Plains Country Towns* (Minneapolis: University of Minnesota Press, 1985), chap. 7, and Hudson, "Towns of the Western Railroads," *Great Plains Quarterly* 2 (Winter 1982): 41–54.

12. Compare town plats in the records held in the courthouses in De Smet, Brookings, Huron, Miller, Highmore, and Pierre.

13. "Town Lot Record Book No. 1, Kingsbury County, 1879–1887," pp. 3–4, Kingsbury County Courthouse, De Smet, South Dakota.

14. Hudson, in *Plains Country Towns*, p. 88, notes this general lack of parks and public meeting places in railroad plats for that area of North Dakota.

15. Edward T. Price, "The Central Courthouse Square in the American County Seat," *Geographical Review* 58 (January 1968): 29–60.

16. De Smet *Leader*, November 17, 1883.

17. Ibid., June 9, 1883; Caryl Lynn Meyer Poppen, ed., *De Smet: Yesterday and Today* (De Smet: De Smet Bicentennial Committee, 1976), pp. 128–29.

18. For more information on railroad stations, see H. Roger Grant and Charles W. Bohi, *The Country Railroad Station in America* (Boulder, Colo.: Pruett, 1978), chap. 3, and Bohi and

Grant, "Country Railroad Stations of the Milwaukee Road and the Chicago and North Western in South Dakota," *South Dakota History* 9 (Winter 1978): 1–23.

19. LIW, *Little Town on the Prairie* (New York: Harper and Row, 1941), pp. 243–51.

20. De Smet *Leader*, March 31, April 14, May 26, 1883.

21. Ibid., March 10, April 21, July 21, August 11, 1883.

22. Ibid., July 21, 1883.

23. Carole Rifkind, *Main Street: The Face of Urban America* (New York: Harper and Row, 1977), pp. 31, 43.

24. LIW, *Little Town on the Prairie*, pp. 50–51, 201–9; De Smet *News*, June 21, 1938.

25. LIW, *The Long Winter:* (New York: Harper and Row, 1940), pp. 91–92. Comparing this list with the 1883 map of the city, we can see that Wilder's memory of Main Street was fairly accurate.

26. Ibid., pp. 18, 127, 140, 157, 261–62, 302.

27. De Smet *Leader*, October 20, 27, November 17, 1883; LIW, *These Happy Golden Years* (New York: Harper and Row, 1943), pp. 165, 181, 284; De Smet *News*, July 15, 1921.

28. De Smet *Leader*, February 17, April 21, 28, August 4, 1883; LIW, *Little Town on the Prairie*, pp. 210–20.

29. De Smet *Leader*, February 17, 24, March 10, April 21, 1883.

30. LIW, *Little Town on the Prairie*, pp. 275–77. In 1884, Reverend Brown retired from the active ministry after serving four years in De Smet (De Smet *Leader*, August 9, 1884).

31. De Smet *Leader*, December 29, 1883.

Chapter 3. Freedom and Control in Fact and Fiction

1. The novels focused upon in this chapter are the five that are set in and around De Smet.

2. LIW, *By the Shores of Silver Lake* (New York: Harper and Row, 1939), p. 4.

3. LIW, *These Happy Golden Years* (New York: Harper and Row, 1943), p. 138.

4. Frederick Jackson Turner established the framework for serious study of the frontier character in "The Significance of the Frontier in American History" (1893), reprinted in *Frontier and Section: Selected Essays of Frederick Jackson Turner*, ed. Ray Allen Billington (Englewood Cliffs, N.J.: Prentice-Hall, 1961), pp. 37–62. Turner and his followers concentrated almost entirely on the male frontier experience, and only in the last two decades

has much attention been paid to the experience of pioneer women. See, for example, Glenda Riley, *Frontierswoman: The Iowa Experience* (Ames: Iowa State University Press, 1981); Joanna L. Stratton, *Pioneer Women: Voices from the Kansas Frontier* (New York: Simon and Schuster, 1981); and Julie Roy Jeffrey, *Frontier Women: The Trans-Mississippi West, 1840–1880* (New York: Hill and Wang, 1979).

5. LIW, *The Long Winter* (New York: Harper and Row, 1940), p. 65; LIW, *These Happy Golden Years*, pp. 153, 169, 196, 269.

6. LIW, *Little Town on the Prairie* (New York: Harper and Row, 1941), pp. 11–12. Rosa Ann Moore shows that Wilder in different scenes reassigned the two girls' attributes so as to maintain consistency in their characters. Thus, while in real life Laura and Mary played sometimes contradictory roles, in the books Mary remained good, patient, and literal while Laura was reckless, restless, and metaphoric ("Laura Ingalls Wilder's Orange Notebooks and the Art of the Little House Books," *Children's Literature* 4 [1975]: 114–15).

7. LIW, *These Happy Golden Years*, p. 138.

8. Ibid., p. 139.

9. Turner, "The Significance of the Frontier," p. 37.

10. Ibid., pp. 56–58, 61–62.

11. Alexis de Tocqueville, *Democracy in America*, ed. J. P. Mayer and Max Lerner, trans. George Lawrence (New York: Harper and Row, 1966), pp. 477–78, and Robert Bellah et al., *Habits of the Heart: Individualism and Commitment in American Life* (New York: Harper and Row, 1986), p. vii.

12. Beard recounted by George W. Pierson, "Turner's Views Challenged," in Ray Allen Billington, ed., *The Frontier Thesis: Valid Interpretation of American History?* (New York: Holt, Rinehart and Winston, 1966), p. 36, and Billington, *America's Frontier Heritage* (New York: Holt, Rinehart and Winston, 1966), p. 53.

13. LIW, *The Long Winter*, p. 209.

14. This account is in ibid., pp. 264–308.

15. De Smet *News*, May 25, October 26, 1900; March 8, 1907; May 17, 1918; October 14, 1921.

16. LIW, *Little Town on the Prairie*, p. 29.

17. Ibid., p. 265; LIW, *The Long Winter*, pp. 187, 288; LIW, *These Happy Golden Years*, p. 197; LIW, *The First Four Years* (New York: Harper and Row, 1971), pp. 38–40, 76–77. See also Doris Rosenblum, " 'Intimate Immensity': Mythic Space in the Works of Laura Ingalls Wilder," in Arthur R. Huseboe and William Geyer, eds., *Where the West Begins: Essays on the Middle*

Border and Siouxland Writing (Sioux Falls, S.Dak.: Center for Western Studies Press, 1978), pp. 72–79.

18. LIW, *The First Four Years*, pp. 104–6; LIW, *Little Town on the Prairie*, p. 102.

19. De Smet *Leader*, March 10, 1883.

20. LIW, *These Happy Golden Years*, p. 197.

21. LIW, *The First Four Years*, pp. 119–20.

22. Anderson, "Literary Apprenticeship of Laura Ingalls Wilder," pp. 290–99; William Holtz, "Closing the Circle: The American Optimism of Laura Ingalls Wilder," *Great Plains Quarterly* 4 (Spring 1984): p. 85.

23. LIW, *The Long Winter*, pp. 192–93.

24. Ibid., pp. 5–10, 107–110, 173, 186, 189, 195; LIW, *The First Four Years*, p. 64.

25. LIW, *By the Shores of Silver Lake*, p. 243; LIW, *Little Town on the Prairie*, pp. 37, 48 (quoted); LIW, *These Happy Golden Years*, pp. 42, 151, 237.

26. On the work ethic, see Daniel T. Rodgers, *The Work Ethic in Industrial America*, 1850–1920 (Chicago: University of Chicago Press, 1974), and Irvin G. Wyllie, *The Self-Made Man in America: The Myth of Rags to Riches* (New York: Free Press, 1954).

27. LIW, *By the Shores of Silver Lake*, p. 237; LIW, *These Happy Golden Years*, p. 119.

28. William T. Anderson, *The Story of the Ingalls* (De Smet, S.Dak.: Laura Ingalls Wilder Memorial Society, 1971), pp. 14–15.

29. LIW, *The First Four Years*, pp. 133–34.

30. LIW, *These Happy Golden Years*, pp. 2–4.

31. LIW, *Little Town on the Prairie*, pp. 97, 184, 228.

32. Ibid., pp. 73–75, 253, 262, 304; LIW, *The Long Winter*, pp. 81, 228; LIW, *These Happy Golden Years*, pp. 24, 98.

33. LIW, *Little Town on the Prairie*, p. 55. Although Kingsbury County in 1883 became the first county under territorial law to vote no license for saloons, the law was very casually enforced, if at all. "There is room for some vigorous temperance work in De Smet," editor Mark Brown commented. "Drunken men reeling and yelling in the streets rather give away a temperance community. The liquid damnation is obtained freely somewhere. It wants looking after" (De Smet *Leader*, March 24 and May 5, 1883).

34. John E. Miller, "The Old-fashioned Fourth of July: A Photographic Essay in Small-town Celebrations Prior to 1930," *South Dakota History* 17 (Summer 1987): 118–39.

35. LIW, *Little Town on the Prairie* draft, pp. 28–32, Pomona, California, Public Library.

36. LIW, *Little Town on the Prairie*, pp. 63–77.

Chapter 4. Love and Affection in Wilder's Life and Writing

1. LIW to RWL, January 26, 1938, Box 13, Lane Papers.

2. LIW and RWL, *A Little House Sampler*, ed. William T. Anderson (Lincoln: University of Nebraska Press, 1988), p. 220.

3. Wilder talked about doing an adult novel during late 1937. LIW to RWL on back of letter from Ida Louise Raymond to LIW, December 18, 1937; RWL to LIW, December 20, 1937, Box 13, Lane Papers. See William Holtz, *The Ghost in the Little House: A Biography of Rose Wilder Lane* (Columbia: University of Missouri Press, 1993), p. 218; William T. Anderson, "The Literary Apprenticeship of Laura Ingalls Wilder," *South Dakota History* 13 (Winter 1983): 290–99.

4. LIW, *These Happy Golden Years* (New York: Harper and Row, 1943), pp. 213–14.

5. LIW, *By the Shores of Silver Lake* (New York: Harper and Row, 1939), pp. 5, 261; LIW, *The Long Winter* (New York: Harper and Row, 1940), p. 65; LIW, *These Happy Golden Years*, pp. 153, 168.

6. LIW, *The Long Winter* (New York: Harper and Row, 1939), p. 4; LIW, "Pioneer Girl" (Brandt version), pp. 91, 111, 113, 138.

7. LIW, *Little Town on the Prairie* (New York: Harper and Row, 1935), p. 90; LIW, "Pioneer Girl" (Brandt version), p. 137. Lane added the part in *The Long Winter* (p. 33) about Laura's not liking to sew; this was not stated in Wilder's original manuscript of the book (p. 24).

8. LIW, *These Happy Golden Years*, pp. 5–12, 21–22, 46–47, 63, 66.

9. LIW, "Pioneer Girl" (Brandt version), p. 124.

10. De Smet *Leader*, July 19, 1884.

11. Donald Zochert, *Laura: The Life of Laura Ingalls Wilder* (New York: Avon, 1977), p. 161; LIW, *Little Town on the Prairie*, p. 45.

12. LIW, "Pioneer Girl" draft. They stayed with the girls when Ma and Pa took Mary to the school for the blind in Vinton, Iowa.

13. LIW, "Pioneer Girl" (Bye version), pp. 125–26; LIW to RWL, Mar. 7, 1938, Box 13, Lane Papers.

14. LIW, *By the Shores of Silver Lake*, pp. 183–85, 195; LIW, *Little Town on the Prairie*, pp. 29, 57, 60, 240–51; LIW, *These Happy Golden Years*, pp. 114–22.

15. On women's roles and the doctrine of separate spheres in the nineteenth century, see Barbara Welter, "The Cult of True Womanhood: 1820–1860," *American Quarterly* 18 (Summer 1966): 151–74; Nancy F. Cott, *The Bonds of Womanhood: "Woman's Sphere" in New England, 1780–1835* (New Haven, Conn.: Yale University Press, 1977); Carl N. Degler, *At Odds: Women and the Family in America from the Revolution to the Present* (New York: Oxford University Press, 1980), chap. 2; Mary P. Ryan, *Womanhood in America: From Colonial Times to the Present*, 3d ed. (New York: Franklin Watts, 1983), pp. 113–29; Karen Lystra, *Women, Men, and Romantic Love in Nineteenth-Century America* (New York: Oxford University Press, 1989), chap. 3; and Glenna Matthews, *"Just a Housewife": The Rise and Fall of Domesticity in America* (New York: Oxford University Press, 1987), pp. 3–66.

16. Francesca M. Cancian, *Love in America: Gender and Self-development* (Cambridge: Cambridge University Press, 1987), pp. 15–65; Lystra, *Women, Men, and Romantic Love in Nineteenth-Century America*, esp. chap. 2; Ellen K. Rothman, *Hands and Hearts: A History of Courtship in America* (New York: Basic Books, 1984), pp. 103–14; Degler, *At Odds: Women and the Family in America from the Revolution to the Present*, pp. 14–25. A dissenting view is expressed in Helen E. Fisher, *Anatomy of Love: The Natural History of Monogamy, Adultery, and Divorce* (New York: Norton, 1992), pp. 49–50.

17. LIW, *The Long Winter*, pp. 3–10, 77–78. *The Long Winter* simplifies events, because it shows Laura alone breaking social conventions in playing ball with the boys while the other girls just look on (pp. 77–78). But in "Pioneer Girl," a more spontaneous and less literary expression of her recollections, Wilder noted that Ida Brown and Mary Power had both joined in playing ball with the boys (LIW, "Pioneer Girl" [Brandt version], p. 119).

18. LIW, *Little Town on the Prairie*, pp. 93–94, 271; LIW, *These Happy Golden Years*, pp. 162, 268–70.

19. LIW, *These Happy Golden Years*, p. 136; LIW, "Pioneer Girl" (Bye version), p. 143; LIW, *Little Town on the Prairie*, pp. 129, 149, 271. Writing to Lane in 1937 on the back of a letter sent to her by Helen Stratte (December 17, 1937), Wilder stated: "I am so surprised she said I was good looking. I always thought I was the homeliest girl ever and the only way I could endure myself was

because I could outdo the boys at their games and forget that I wasn't pretty. Funny!" (Lane Papers, Box 13).

20. LIW, "Pioneer Girl" (Bye version), pp. 142-43; LIW, *The Long Winter*, pp. 19-24.

21. LIW, *Little Town on the Prairie*, pp. 197-200; LIW, "Pioneer Girl" (Bye version), p. 160.

22. LIW, *The Long Winter*, p. 99; LIW, "Pioneer Girl" (Bye version), p. 164.

23. LIW, *By the Shores of Silver Lake*, pp. 49-50; LIW to RWL, March 7, 1938, Box 13, Lane Papers.

24. LIW, "Pioneer Girl" (Bye version), pp. 149-50, 164; LIW, *These Happy Golden Years*, p. 170.

25. LIW, "Pioneer Girl" (Bye version), pp. 136, 149, 150.

26. Donald Zochert, *Laura: The Life of Laura Ingalls Wilder* (New York: Avon, 1977), pp. 154, 166. Chapter 9 of *The Long Winter* is entitled "Cap Garland." Lane probably gave it this title, because the original draft of the chapter was called "Going to School." The other character in the series to have a chapter named after him or her was Nellie Oleson, who got two: chapter 21 of *By the Banks of Plum Creek* and chapter 20 of *These Happy Golden Years*. Characters mentioned in chapter titles were Mary Ingalls in two, Almanzo Wilder in two, and Eliza Wilder in one.

27. LIW, *The Long Winter*, pp. 77-78, 89.

28. LIW, *These Happy Golden Years*, p. 77.

29. LIW, "Pioneer Girl" (Bye version), p. 151; LIW, *Little Town on the Prairie*, pp. 179-80.

30. LIW, *These Happy Golden Years*, pp. 77, 92; LIW, "Pioneer Girl" (Bye version), p. 164.

31. LIW, "Pioneer Girl" draft; LIW, *These Happy Golden Years*, p. 90; LIW, "Pioneer Girl" (Brandt version), p. 132; LIW, "Pioneer Girl" (Bye version), p. 159. In the first draft of *These Happy Golden Years* (p. 83), Wilder reinjected some longing for Cap: "Mary Power and Cap Garland went by in a cutter built for two. Laura wished the cutter had been larger and they had taken her with them."

32. LIW, "Pioneer Girl" (Bye version), p. 143; LIW, *Little Town on the Prairie*, p. 129. While she was planning the concluding volume of the series, *Prairie Girl*, which later was split into two books, Wilder wrote Lane: "I think I will let Nellie Olson take Jennie Masters' place in Prairie Girl and let her be the only girl from Plum Creek. Their characters were alike" (LIW to RWL, March 15, 1938, Box 13, Lane Papers). Later she wrote, "I think I'll combine Jennie Masters and Stella [Gilbert] in Nellie Olson" (LIW to RWL, August 17, 1938, Box 13, Lane Papers).

33. LIW, "Pioneer Girl" (Bye version), pp. 176-78; LIW, *These Happy Golden Years*, chap. 20.

34. Robert C. Solomon, *About Love: Reinventing Romance for Our Time* (New York: Simon and Schuster, 1988), p. 35. See also Elaine Walster and G. William Walster, *A New Look at Love* (Reading, Mass.: Addison-Wesley, 1978), pp. 8, 40-45.

35. LIW to RWL, January 25, 1938, Box 13, Lane Papers. Wilder noted that she was "shy" about talking about the opposite sex in *These Happy Golden Years*, pp. 136, 169, 216. Lane wrote to her friend Guy Moyston about her mother, "She hates anything at all that has to do in any way with sex" (quoted in Holtz, *The Ghost in the Little House*, p. 153).

36. Degler, *At Odds: Women and the Family in America from the Revolution to the Present*, pp. 249-50; LIW, *These Happy Golden Years*, p. 166. The anecdote about Almanzo's fear that Laura wouldn't want to kiss him on their engagement night, described in "Pioneer Girl" (Bye version, p. 191), was omitted from *These Happy Golden Years*, p. 216.

37. LIW, proposed outline for "Prairie Girl," Folder 243, Box 16, Lane Papers.

38. LIW, *These Happy Golden Years*, p. 230.

Chapter 5. Fact and Interpretation in Wilder's Fiction

1. Joseph Brent, *Charles Sanders Peirce: A Biography* (Bloomington: Indiana University Press, 1993). John K. Sheriff, *The Fate of Meaning: Charles Peirce, Structuralism, and Literature* (Princeton, N.J.: Princeton University Press, 1989). The quotation is from *The Collected Papers of Charles Sanders Peirce*, vols. 1-6 ed. Charles Hartshorne and Paul Weiss; vols. 7-8 ed. Arthur W. Burks (Cambridge, Mass.: Harvard University Press, 1931-58), 2.228 (the first numeral refers to the volume number and the numeral to the right of the point refers to the paragraph).

2. *The Collected Papers of Charles Sanders Peirce*, 8.314; David Savan, *An Introduction to C. S. Peirce's Semiotics* (Toronto: Victoria University, 1976), p. 16; Michael Shapiro, *The Sense of Grammar: Language as Semeiotic* (Bloomington: Indiana University Press, 1983), pp. 36-37. Although Peirce denied that semiosis necessarily had to be connected to human beings, he admitted that for most people it does involve a person upon whose consciousness sign action produces an interpretant if the process is to be intelligible to them (*Semiotics and Significs:*

The Correspondence between Charles S. Peirce and Victoria Lady Welby, ed. Charles S. Hardwick [Bloomington: Indiana University Press, 1977], pp. 80–81.

3. *The Collected Papers of Charles Sanders Peirce*, 5.448n.

4. Ray Allen Billington, *Land of Savagery, Land of Promise: The European Image of the American Frontier in the Nineteenth Century* (New York: Norton, 1981), esp. chaps. 2, 12; Herbert S. Schell, *History of South Dakota* (Lincoln: University of Nebraska Press, 1975), pp. 161–68; Kenneth Hammer, "Dakota Railroads" (Ph.D. dissertation, South Dakota State University, 1966), pp. 183–200; Robert J. Casey and W. A. S. Douglas, *Pioneer Railroad: The Story of the Chicago and North Western System* (New York: Whittlesey House, 1948), pp. 161–66.

5. Lewis Atherton, *Main Street on the Middle Border* (Bloomington: Indiana Univeresity Press, 1954); Everett Dick, *The Sod-House Frontier, 1854–1890* (New York: Appleton-Century, 1937), esp. chap. 26.

6. LIW, *By the Shores of Silver Lake* (New York: Harper and Row, 1939), p. 222; LIW, *Little Town on the Prairie* (New York: Harper and Row, 1941), p. 27; LIW, *Long Winter* (New York: Harper and Row, 1940), p. 127.

7. LIW, *Long Winter*, pp. 305–6. The Loftus incident, which took about a single page to describe in Wilder's original draft (p. 247), was expanded into six pages for the final version of the book.

8. See De Smet *Leader*, various issues, 1883.

9. LIW, *Long Winter*, p. 169.

10. Janet Spaeth, *Laura Ingalls Wilder* (Boston: Twayne, 1987), chap. 2.

11. LIW, *By the Shores of Silver Lake*, p. 237; LIW, *Long Winter*, p. 26. In the first instance, Laura included the slogan in her original draft. In the second, it was added during the editing process.

12. LIW, *Little Town on the Prairie*, p. 102; LIW, *Long Winter*, pp. 118, 222.

13. LIW, *Long Winter*, p. 196; LIW, *By the Shores of Silver Lake*, p. 5; LIW, *Little Town on the Prairie*, p. 107; LIW, *These Happy Golden Years* (New York: Harper and Row, 1943), pp. 235, 271.

14. LIW, *These Happy Golden Years*, p. 289.

15. LIW, *Long Winter*, p. 37.

16. Ibid., p. 241.

17. LIW, *By the Shores of Silver Lake*, pp. 213, 290; LIW, *These Happy Golden Years*, p. 277.

18. LIW, *Little Town on the Prairie*, p. 182.

19. LIW, *These Happy Golden Years*, pp. 17, 27.

20. Shapiro, *The Sense of Grammar*, p. 7.

21. LIW, "Pioneer Girl" (Bye version), p. 141.

22. LIW, *Little Town on the Prairie*, p. 274.

23. Ibid., p. 48; LIW, *These Happy Golden Years*, p. 260.

24. LIW, *By the Shores of Silver Lake*, pp. 59, 65, 66, 72.

25. LIW, *Long Winter*, pp. 16, 68, 75, 125; LIW, *Little Town on the Prairie*, pp. 2, 37, 49, 97, 261; LIW, *These Happy Golden Years*, p. 37.

26. LIW, *These Happy Golden Years*, p. 199; De Smet *Leader*, September 13, October 4, 18, 1884.

Chapter 6. Narrative Rules and the Process of Storytelling

1. LIW, "Detroit Book Week Speech," 1937, Box 14, Lane Papers. This speech is reprinted in LIW and RWL, *A Little House Sampler*, William T. Anderson, ed. (Lincoln: University of Nebraska Press, 1988), pp. 216–24.

2. William T. Anderson, "The Literary Apprenticeship of Laura Ingalls Wilder," *South Dakota History* 13 (Winter 1983): 285–331; William Holtz, *The Ghost in the Little House: A Life of Rose Wilder Lane* (Columbia: University of Missouri Press, 1993), pp. 220–26.

3. LIW and RWL, *Little House Sampler*, p. 216.

4. LIW, *The Long Winter* (New York: Harper and Row, 1940), pp. 40, 97, 173, 185, 215; LIW, *Little Town on the Prairie* (New York: Harper and Row, 1941), p. 110; LIW, *These Happy Golden Years* (New York: Harper and Row, 1943), p. 43.

5. LIW, "Pioneer Girl" (Brandt version), pp. 12, 29.

6. LIW, *Little Town on the Prairie*, pp. 72–73.

7. David Carr, *Time, Narrative, and History* (Bloomington: Indiana University Press, 1991), p. 71; Alasdair MacIntyre, *After Virtue: A Study in Moral Theory* (Notre Dame: University of Notre Dame Press, 1981), p. 197.

8. Peter Brooks, *Reading for the Plot: Design and Intention in Narrative* (New York: Alfred A. Knopf, 1984), p. 3.

9. LIW to RWL, August 17, 1938, Box 13, Lane Papers.

10. LIW, *The First Four Years* (New York: Harper and Row, 1971), pp. 105–6; Wilder's handwritten notes on the manuscript of *The First Four Years*, Box 16, Lane Papers.

11. LIW to RWL, March 20, 1937, Box 13, Lane Papers.

12. Ibid., August 17, 1938.

13. Ibid., January 25, 1938.

14. Ibid., August 17, 1938.

15. Ibid., March 23, 1937, and undated reply to letter of December 19, 1937; LIW, *By the Shores of Silver Lake* (New York: Harper and Row, 1939), pp. 1-2.

16. LIW to RWL, undated reply to letter of December 19, 1937, Box 13, Lane Papers; LIW, *By the Shores of Silver Lake*, pp. 96-106.

17. LIW, *Little Town on the Prairie*, pp. 35-56; LIW, undated two-page memorandum on her work with Mr. Clayson, Box 13, Lane Papers.

18. LIW to RWL, August 17, 1938, Box 13, Lane Papers; LIW, *These Happy Golden Years*, p. 2.

19. LIW to RWL, August 17, 1938, Box 13, Lane Papers.

20. De Smet *Leader*, May 31, November 15, 1884.

21. Ibid., March 7, 1938.

22. LIW, *By the Shores of Silver Lake*, pp. 239-40; LIW, *These Happy Golden Years* draft, Detroit Public Library, pp. 304-5; LIW, *These Happy Golden Years*, pp. 280-82

23. LIW to RWL, March 7, 1938, Box 13, Lane Papers.

24. LIW, *Little Town on the Prairie*, pp. 197-200; LIW, *Little Town on the Prairie* draft, pp. 97-98, Pomona, California, Public Library; LIW to RWL, February 19, 1938, Box 13, Lane Papers.

25. RWL to LIW, December 19, 1937, Box 13, Lane Papers.

26. Lane's handwritten notes on draft of *These Happy Golden Years*, p. 77, Box 16, Lane Papers; LIW, *These Happy Golden Years*, p. 100.

27. LIW, "Pioneer Girl" draft.

28. LIW, *By the Shores of Silver Lake* manuscript, pp. 5-6.

29. LIW, *By the Shores of Silver Lake*, p. 21.

30. LIW, *Little Town on the Prairie*, pp. 73-77; Rose Wilder Lane, "Credo," *Saturday Evening Post*, March 7, 1936, pp. 5-7, 30-35; Holtz, *The Ghost in the Little House*, pp. 382-83.

31. RWL to LIW, December 19, 1937; LIW to RWL, undated response to previous letter, Box 13, Lane Papers.

32. RWL to LIW, no date [late October, 1937], Box 13, Lane Papers.

33. Ibid., December 19, 1937; LIW to RWL, undated response to previous letter, January 25, 1938, January 28, 1938; LIW, Notes on "Silver Lake," no date.

34. LIW to RWL, February 19, 1938, Box 13, Lane Papers.

35. Ibid., January 25, 1938.

36. Ibid., February 19, 1938.

37. Janet Spaeth, *Laura Ingalls Wilder* (Boston: Twayne, 1987), p. 71–73.

38. RWL to LIW, December 19, 1937, Box 13, Lane Papers.

39. LIW to RWL, January 26, 1938. Box 13, Lane Papers.

40. Ibid., August 17, 1938.

Chapter 7. Textbook History versus Lived History

1. LIW and RWL, *A Little House Sampler*, ed. William T. Anderson (Lincoln: University of Nebraska Press, 1988), p. 217.

2. Ibid.

3. Elsie A. Nickel to LIW, March 1, 1935; Donna Anderson to LIW, May 13, 1948; sixth-grade class, Longfellow School, La Crosse, Wis., to LIW, January 6, 1947, Mail from Fans, 1933–1949, Box 14, Lane Papers.

4. Donna Anderson to LIW, May 13, 1948; Katherine Afonin to LIW, May 28, 1949, Mail from Fans, 1933–1949, Box 14, Lane Papers.

5. Charles Carpenter, *History of American Schoolbooks* (Philadelphia: University of Pennsylvania Press, 1963), pp. 197–99, 204; R. Freeman Butts and Lawrence A. Cremin, *A History of Education in American Culture* (New York: Holt, Rinehart and Winston, 1961), p. 435.

6. *Little Town on the Prairie* (New York: Harper and Row, 1941) placed the school exhibition in December 1882 (pp. 287–95). Wilder's "Pioneer Girl" manuscript, a more directly autobiographical and less artistic telling of the story, dated the exhibition a year later ("Pioneer Girl" [Bye version], pp. 169–70).

7. Laura's exploits became more modest in the published version, which divided the burden evenly between Laura and Ida. In "Pioneer Girl," Laura was assigned two-thirds of the chronology and Ida one-third.

8. LIW, *Little Town on the Prairie*, pp. 290–93.

9. Ruth Miller Elson, *Guardians of Tradition: American Schoolbooks of the Nineteenth Century* (Lincoln: University of Nebraska Press, 1964), p. 8; Francis Fitzgerald, *America Revised: History Textbooks in the Twentieth Century* (New York: Vintage Books, 1980), p. 19.

10. Quoted in Richard Hofstadter, *Anti-intellectualism in American Life* (New York: Knopf, 1963), p. 307.

11. Elson, *Guardians of Tradition*, pp. 186, 266, 282–83, 337–38;

John A. Nietz, *Old Textbooks* (Pittsburgh, Pa.: University of Pittsburgh Press, 1961), pp. 237-39.

12. Edward Taylor, *A Brief Account of the American People for Schools* (Chicago: George Sherwood and Company, 1878), p. 3. Wilder's autographed copy of the textbook is located with her papers in the Rare Book Room of the Detroit Public Library.

13. Ibid., p. 4; Nietz, *Old Textbooks*, pp. 240, 242; Butts and Cremin, *A History of Education in American Culture*, p. 442.

14. Taylor, *Brief Account*, p. 4 (italics in original).

15. Richard Hofstadter, *The Progressive Historians: Turner, Beard, Parrington* (New York: Knopf, 1968).

16. Carl Becker, "Everyman His Own Historian," *American Historical Review* 37 (January 1932): 221-36.

17. Ray Allan Billington, *America's Frontier Heritage* (New York: Holt, Rinehart and Winston, 1966), chap. 1; Billington, *Frederick Jackson Turner; Historian, Scholar, Teacher* (New York: Oxford University Press, 1973), chaps. 5, 8.

18. LIW to RWL, January 25, 1938, Box 13, Lane Papers.

19. RWL to William T. Anderson, June 30, 1966, quoted in Anderson, "The Literary Apprenticeship of Laura Ingalls Wilder," *South Dakota History* 13 (Winter 1983): 288.

20. RWL to William T. Anderson, July 13, 1966, quoted in ibid., pp. 288-89.

21. Wilder's handwritten comments on manuscript of *The Long Winter*, p. 89, Box 15, Lane Papers. Despite their efforts, Wilder and Lane did get this fact wrong. Wilder penciled on the manuscript, "I remember we used to say 60 miles to Brookings. Manly don't remember. As near as I can figure by highway map it is fifty miles." Actually, the distance was closer to forty miles. In the published book (p. 106) the error was compounded by fixing the distance to Volga (which is seven miles west of Brookings) at fifty miles when it was actually closer to thirty-three.

22. RWL to LIW [late October 1937], filed with "Detroit Book Week Speech," Box 14, Lane Papers.

23. RWL to LIW, unattached fragment [early February 1938?], Box 13, Lane Papers.

24. LIW to Martha Carpenter, June 22, 1925, Box 17, Lane Papers.

25. William Anderson, *Laura Ingalls Wilder: A Biography* (New York: HarperCollins, 1992), pp. 196-98, 204-6, 208-9; Wilder's map of De Smet is in the Wilder Papers, Detroit Public Library.

26. LIW to RWL [ca. March 1937], October 8, 1938, Box 13, Lane Papers.

27. Wilder's comments are written on the back of a letter from Helen Stratte to LIW, December 17, 1937, Box 13, Lane Papers.

28. LIW to RWL, February 5, 1937, Box 13, Lane Papers.

29. Edmund Blair Bolles, *Remembering and Forgetting: An Inquiry into the Nature of Memory* (New York: Walker, 1988), p. 181. On the construction of memory, see also David Thelen, "Memory and American History," *Journal of American History* 75 (March 1989): 1119–21; Michael Kammen, *Mystic Chords of Memory: The Transformation of Tradition in American Culture* (New York: Knopf, 1991), pp. 3–4, 17–39; and George Lipsitz, *Time Passages: Collective Memory and American Popular Culture* (Minneapolis: University of Minnesota Press, 1990), p. 34. Frederick C. Bartlett was an early advocate of the notion that memory is a constructive, imaginative process in *Remembering: A Study in Experimental and Social Psychology* (Cambridge: Cambridge University Press, 1932).

30. Pierre Nora, "Between Memory and History: *Les Lieux de Memoire*," *Representations* 25 (Spring 1989): 8.

31. For examples of this process of self-censorship see LIW to RWL, February 5, 1937, Box 13, Lane Papers.

32. RWL Journal, December 23, 1932, Box 22, Lane Papers.

33. RWL, American novel outline, Item 51, Box 23, Lane Papers. These notes were written on January 11, 1933, and later.

34. Awareness of the impracticality of the project came soon. In her journal entry for June 26, 1933, Lane wrote: "Yesterday I worked out the basic plan of the novel—ten books, and suddenly I was overwhelmed with despair. I knew I haven't the powers to do such a thing, and saw myself as the absurd & pitious ambition that attempts and fails to do more than it can. I saw the cheap, thin, wobbling work that will come of all this effort—the smiles of critics and the blank incomprehension of readers. All the rest of the day I was sunk" (RWL Journal, June 26, 1933, Box 23, Lane Papers).

35. William T. Anderson, "Laura Ingalls Wilder and Rose Wilder Lane: The Continuing Collaboration," *South Dakota History* 16 (Summer 1986): 116.

36. For example, see clippings of reviews of *Little Town on the Prairie* in Folder 246, Box 16, Lane Papers. *Child Life* (Chicago, October 1941) said Wilder had written "a collection of stories that are true American history as well as splendid reading." The *New Republic* (December 15, 1941) called the book "a warm, humorous story of real pioneers of the eighties." The New York *World-Telegram* (June 24, 1941) said, "The books are all autobio-

graphical, name real names, and are generally considered to be one of the finest chapters of Americana for children written in our time." The Chicago *News* (November 5, 1941) said Wilder's book added to "her series of true pioneer stories of the Middle West." *Progressive Education* (November 1941) praised Wilder's "realistic picture of early days."

37. Maria Cimino, "Laura Ingalls Wilder," *Wilson Library Bulletin* 22 (April 1948): 582; George McGovern, "A Fine Way Back to Our Prairie Past," *Life*, July 2, 1971, p. 12.

38. C. Vann Woodward, *The Strange Career of Jim Crow* (New York: Oxford University Press, 1955), p. viii.

Chapter 8. De Smet as Frontier Destination and Way Station

1. Frederick Jackson Turner, "The Significance of the Frontier in American History," in *Report of the American Historical Association* for 1893, pp. 199–227. See also Richard Hofstadter and Seymour Martin Lipset, eds., *Turner and the Sociology of the Frontier* (New York: Basic Books, 1968), and Ray Allen Billington, *America's Frontier Heritage* (New York: Holt, Rinehart and Winston, 1966).

2. George W. Pierson, *The Moving American* (New York: Alfred A. Knopf, 1975).

3. Ibid., p. 4; Billington, *America's Frontier Heritage*, pp. 181–89; Barbara Vobejda, "Americans Still on the Move, But Less," Washington *Post*, December 20, 1991, p. A3.

4. LIW to RWL, March 7, 1938, Box 13, Lane Papers.

5. Turner's frontier was largely a male-populated one. On the assumed reluctance of women to join men on the frontier see discussions by Susan Armitage, "Reluctant Pioneers," in Helen Winter Stauffer and Susan J. Rosowski, eds., *Women and Western American Literature* (Troy, N.Y.: Whitson, 1982), pp. 40–51, and Sandra L. Myres, "Women in the West," in Michael P. Malone, ed., *Historians and the American West* (Lincoln: University of Nebraska Press, 1983), pp. 370–71. John C. Hudson provides a useful corrective when he reminds us that the "Daniel Boone syndrome," which is sometimes portrayed as typical on the frontier, was actually an extreme case ("The Study of Western Frontier Populations," in Jerome O. Steffan, ed., *The American West: New Perspectives, New Dimensions* [Norman: University of Oklahoma Press, 1979], p. 39).

6. William T. Anderson, *The Story of the Ingalls* (Davison, Mich.: privately printed, 1971), pp. 16, 26–27, 30; Anderson, *Laura Ingalls Wilder: A Biography* (New York: HarperCollins, 1992), pp. 166–67, 197.

7. LIW, *On the Way Home: The Diary of a Trip from South Dakota to Mansfield, Missouri, in 1894* (New York: Harper and Row, 1962).

8. An exception to this tendency is the work of geographer John C. Hudson—see his articles listed in note 17.

9. The census manuscripts on microfilm are available through the 1920 census (except for 1890) from the National Archives.

10. John C. Hudson, "Yankeeland in the Middle West," *Journal of Geography* 85 (September–October 1986): 195–200.

11. For information on the Yankee cultural hearth and the Yankee migration see Carleton Beals, *Our Yankee Heritage: New England's Contribution to American Civilization* (New York: David McKay, 1955); Stewart Holbrook, *The Yankee Exodus: An Account of Migration from New England* (New York: Macmillan, 1950); and Lois K. Mathews, *The Expansion of New England* (New York: Russell and Russell, 1909).

12. LIW, *The Long Winter* (New York: Harper and Row, 1940), p. 67; De Smet *Leader*, July 7, October 27, 1883; De Smet *News*, April 21, 1911; February 14, 1913; January 5, 1923; *South Dakota Legislative Manual* (1903), pp. 235–36; ibid. (1907), pp. 457–58.

13. The leapfrogging nature of settlement is noted by James C. Malin in *The Grassland of North America: Prolegomena to Its History* (Lawrence, Kans.: privately printed, 1947), p. 288; John C. Hudson, "Two Dakota Homestead Frontiers," *Annals of the Association of American Geographers* 63 (December 1973): 447; and John Fraser Hart, "Facets of the Geography of Population in the Midwest," *Journal of Geography* 85 (September–October 1986): 206.

14. LIW, *Little Town on the Prairie* (New York: Harper and Row, 1941), pp. 240–51; LIW, *The Long Winter*, pp. 84, 92, 98.

15. De Smet *News*, March 5, 1905;, December 29, 1916.

16. Information from census records for 1880, 1900, 1910, and 1920.

17. On the process of migration to Dakota Territory and South Dakota from eastern states and Europe see two articles by Robert C. Ostergren: "Geographic Perspectives on the History of Settlement in the Upper Middle West," *Upper Midwest History* 1

(1981): 27–39, and "European Settlement and Ethnicity Patterns on the Agricultural Frontiers of South Dakota," *South Dakota History* 13 (Spring–Summer 1983): 49–82, and five articles by John C. Hudson: "Two Dakota Homestead Frontiers"; "Migration to an American Frontier," *Annals of the American Association of Geographers* 66 (June 1976): 242–65; "North American Origins of Middlewestern Frontier Populations," ibid. 78 (September 1988): 395–413; "Who Was 'Forest Man?'" *Great Plains Quarterly* 6 (Spring 1986): 69–83; and "The Study of Western Frontier Populations," pp. 35–60.

18. Settlers on the frontier were generally younger on average than people living in settled areas, but the gap between the two groups was not overwhelming. See Glenda Riley, *The Female Frontier: A Comparative View of Women on the Prairie and the Plains* (Lawrence: University Press of Kansas, 1988), p. 23; Allan G. Bogue, *From Prairie to Corn Belt: Farming on the Illinois and Iowa Prairies in the Nineteenth Century* (Chicago: Quadrangle Books, 1968), pp. 21–24; and Hudson, "The Study of Western Frontier Populations," pp. 43–45.

19. The large number of persons in the twenty-to-twenty-nine age category conforms to the results of Jack E. Eblen's study of frontier populations based on census data from 1840, 1850, and 1860, "An Analysis of Nineteenth-Century Frontier Populations," *Demography* 2 (1965): 399–413. Glenda Riley notes that lopsided gender ratios usually evened out quickly (*Female Frontier*, pp. 15, 18). See also Hudson, "The Study of Western Frontier Populations," pp. 43–45, 48–50.

20. Anderson, *Laura Ingalls Wilder: A Biography*, pp. 166–67; De Smet *News*, March 31, August 18, 1916.

21. Ibid., January 2, 1915; August 10, 1917; March 27, 1925.

22. Ibid., July 15, 1921.

23. Ibid., September 2, 1910; December 3, 1915; December 22, 1916.

24. LIW, *The Long Winter*, pp. 305–6.

25. De Smet *News*, October 26, 1900; March 8, 1907; October 14, 1921; October 12, 1923.

26. Ibid., February 24, 1922.

27. Kenneth A. Schaack, "George W. Hopp: Brookings *County Press* 1879–1890" (Master's thesis, South Dakota State University, 1969), pp. 13, 25, 54; Robert F. Karolevitz, *With a Shirt Tail Full of Type: The Story of Newspapering in South Dakota* (Freeman, S.Dak.: South Dakota Press Association, 1982), pp. 28, 80; Donald Zochert, *Laura: The Life of Laura Ingalls Wilder*

(New York: Avon, 1977), p. 143; De Smet *Leader*, September 6, 1890; De Smet *News*, March 9, 1900.

28. De Smet *News*, January 7, 1921; February 16, April 20, 1923; August 13, 1926.

29. LIW, *Little Town on the Prairie*, p. 71; De Smet *News*, February 2, 1917; May 26, September 22, 1922; October 3, 1924.

30. De Smet *News*, January 12, 19, 26, 1917; December 2, 9, 16, 23, 30, 1921.

31. The popularity of Chicago, the Twin Cities, Seattle, Portland, San Francisco, Los Angeles, and San Diego as destinations for former Dakotans is also noted by John Hudson in "The Study of Western Frontier Populations." Compare his map of 1939 residences of children of North Dakota pioneers on pp. 52–53.

32. William Holtz, *The Ghost in the Little House: A Life of Rose Wilder Lane* (Columbia: University of Missouri Press, 1993); William T. Anderson, *Laura's Rose: The Story of Rose Wilder Lane* (De Smet, S.Dak.: Laura Ingalls Wilder Memorial Society, 1976).

Chapter 9. Relaxing and Building Community at the Couse Opera House

1. Lewis Atherton, *Main Street on the Middle Border* (Bloomington: Indiana University Press, 1954), pp. 135–42; Richard Lingeman, *Small Town America: A Narrative History, 1620–the Present* (New York: G. P. Putnam's Sons, 1980), pp. 300–303; Harold E. Briggs and Ernestine Bennett Briggs, "The Early Theatre on the Northern Plains," *Mississippi Valley Historical Review* 37 (September, 1950): 231–64. On opera houses in South Dakota, see Judith K. Zivanovic, ed., *Opera Houses of the Midwest* (N.p.: Mid-America Theatre Conference, 1988); Gerry A. Perrin, "A History of the Theatrical and Community Activities in the Early Dell Rapids, South Dakota, Opera House" (Master's thesis, South Dakota State University, 1970); and Theodore R. Switzer, "A History of Theatre and Theatrical Activities in Brookings, South Dakota, from 1879 through 1898" (Master's thesis, South Dakota State College, 1962).

2. De Smet *Leader*, December 11, 1886.

3. Ibid., January 27, April 21, December 8, 1883.

4. Ibid., September 2, 1883; August 9, October 25, November 15, 1884; March 27, 1886.

5. Ibid., July 7, December 8, 15, 22, 1883.

6. Ibid., March 7, May 9, December 5, 1885; June 19, October

30, 1886; April 23, May 21, 1887. Wilder included a description of a New England supper in her draft of Little Town on the Prairie (chap. 13), Pomona, California, Public Library, but it was eliminated during the editing process.

7. Ibid., November 15, 1884; October 9, 16, 1886.

8. Wilder, Little Town on the Prairie (New York: Harper and Row, 1941), pp. 207–8, 276–78; These Happy Golden Years (New York: Harper and Row, 1943), pp. 42, 164; De Smet Leader, November 10, 17, 1883; March 19, 1887.

9. De Smet Leader, November 21, 18, 1885; January 23, 1886; April 9, July 16, October 1, 1887.

10. Ibid., January 15, 1887; De Smet News, October 30, 1903; December 2, 1904; March 17, May 26, 1905; February 9, 1906; January 1, 1909; February 20, October 2, 1914; April 9, November 12, 1915; February 10, 1922; October 8, 1926; September 16, 1927; June 14, 1929; January 3, June 6, 1930; March 18, 1932.

11. De Smet News, March 18, 1943.

12. De Smet Leader, March 13, 1886; Wilder, Little Town on the Prairie, pp. 216–20.

13. De Smet News, December 9, 1910; February 11, 1916; March 24, 1922; June 6, 1940.

14. Everett Dick, The Sod-House Frontier, 1865–1890 (New York: D. A. Appleton-Century, 1937); Atherton, Main Street on the Middle Border; Lingeman, Small Town America.

15. De Smet Leader, February 17, 1883; January–April 1886.

16. Ibid., March 14, 1885; December 26, 1886.

17. Ibid., March 14, 1885.

18. Ibid., March 10, November 17, 1883; September 20, 1884; November 28, 1885; March 20, 1886; De Smet News, November 23, 1906; December 10, 1920.

19. De Smet Leader, August 11, 1883; June 5, 12, 16, 1886.

20. Ibid., April 21, June 2, 16, July 7, 14, 1883; August 16, September 20, Nov. 15, 1884; April 11, June 13, November 14, December 5, 1885; April 5, November 6, 30, 1886.

21. LIW, "Pioneer Girl" (Brandt version), p. 153; Harrold (S. Dak.) Star, September 11, November 21, 28, 1884; De Smet Leader, January 5, July 26, 1884; March 14, May 2, 16, 23, October 17, 1885; March 6, 1886; April 26, May 1, November 6, 1886; January 22, 1887.

22. LIW, "Pioneer Girl" (Bye version), pp. 108–9; LIW to RWL, August 17, 1938, Box 13, Lane Papers. Couse's store is mentioned in The Long Winter (New York: Harper and Row, 1940), pp. 92, 98.

23. De Smet *Leader*, April 9, 23, 1887; February 8, April 25, July 19, 1890; De Smet *News*, December 22, 1916.

24. De Smet *Leader*, April 4, 1885; January 30, April 17, 24, October 9, 1886.

25. Ibid., November 13, 1886.

26. Ibid., October 9, November 13, 1886; January 15, 1887.

27. This entire account is from ibid., November 13, 1886.

28. Ibid., January 1, 15, 29, February 5, March 26, April 2, 9, May 7, 1887.

29. Ibid., January 29, February 5, 19, 1887; Philip C. Lewis, *Trouping: How the Show Came to Town* (New York: Harper and Row, 1973), pp. 86–87.

30. De Smet *Leader*, March 12, 1887.

31. De Smet *Leader*, May 14, 21, 1887; De Smet *News*, May 1, 1908; September 9, 1910; July 2, 1915; Lewis, *Trouping*, pp. 66–74; Richard Moody, "Uncle Tom, the Theatre and Mrs. Stowe," *American Heritage* 6 (October 1955): 102–3.

32. De Smet *Leader*, May 14, June 11, July 16, 1887; July 19, August 9, 1890; De Smet *News*, April 3, 1908; May 3, 1918.

33. The quotation is from the De Smet *News*, September 29, 1916. See also issues of February 11, September 15, 22, 1916; March 30, 1917; April 11, 1919.

34. Lewis, *Trouping*, pp. 226–28; De Smet *News*, December 13, 1918; May 2, 1919; April 2, 1916; March 28, April 11, 1930.

35. De Smet *News*, March 18, 1910.

36. Ibid., December 8, 22, 1916; January 5, 1917; May 13, 1927; Caryl Lynn Meyer Poppen, *De Smet: Yesterday and Today* (De Smet: De Smet Bicentennial Committee, 1976), pp. 392–93.

37. De Smet *News*, March 18, October 28, November 4, 1910; March 10, 1911; January 2, 1914; February 11, 1916; Poppen, *De Smet: Yesterday and Today*, p. 326; Alice and Walt Klinkel, interview with the author, De Smet, June 23, 1982.

38. Poppen, *De Smet: Yesterday and Today*, pp. 343–44.

39. Wilder, *Long Winter*, pp. 59, 127, 137, 140, 147, 157, 243–44, 261.

40. Wilder, *Little Town on the Prairie*, pp. 27, 71.

41. Ibid., pp. 213–20, 223, 233; De Smet *Leader*, February 17, 24, 1883; January 30, February 6, 13, March 20, 27, 1886.

42. Wilder, *Little Town on the Prairie*, p. 237; De Smet *Leader*, March 14, 1885.

43. Wilder, *Little Town on the Prairie*, p. 239.

44. Ibid., pp. 256–60, 273–97; *These Happy Golden Years*, pp. 146, 199–208.

Chapter 10. Two Artists of the Prairie

1. On the South Dakota prairie landscape, see John Milton, *South Dakota* (New York: Norton, 1977), chap. 5; David Allen Evans, *What the Tallgrass Says* (Sioux Falls: Center for Western Studies, 1982); and David J. Holden, *Dakota Visions: A County Approach* (Sioux Falls: Center for Western Studies, 1982). See also Walter Prescott Webb, *The Great Plains* (Boston: Ginn, 1931); Carl F. Kraenzel, *The Great Plains in Transition* (Norman: University of Oklahoma Press, 1955); J. E. Weaver, *Prairie Plants and Their Environment: A Fifty-Year Study in the Midwest* (Lincoln: University of Nebraska Press, 1968); and David Lowenthal, "The Pioneer Landscape: An American Dream," *Great Plains Quarterly* 2 (Winter 1982): 5–19.

2. Willa Cather, *My Antonia* (Boston: Houghton Mifflin, 1918), p. 7. On literary and artistic responses to the landscape of the American West, see Henry Nash Smith, *Virgin Land: The American West as Symbol and Myth* (Cambridge, Mass.: Harvard University Press, 1950); Howard Mumford Jones, *O Strange New World: American Culture: the Formative Years* (New York: Viking, 1964), chap. 10; Robert Thacker, *The Great Prairie Fact and Literary Imagination* (Albuquerque: University of New Mexico Press, 1989); and Annette Kolodny, *The Lay of the Land: Metaphor as Experience and History in American Life and Letters* (Chapel Hill: University of North Carolina Press, 1975), chap. 4.

3. LIW, *By the Shores of Silver Lake* (New York: Harper and Row, 1939), p. 37.

4. Ibid., pp. 38, 60.

5. William Least Heat-Moon's *PrairyErth (a deep map)* (Boston: Houghton Mifflin, 1991) eloquently disproves the notion that there is anything simple about the prairie environment.

6. Ole E. Rolvaag, *Giants in the Earth: A Saga of the Prairie* (New York: Harper and Row, 1929); Hamlin Garland, *Main-Traveled Roads* (New York: Harper, 1899) and *A Son of the Middle Border* (New York: Grosset and Dunlap, 1917).

7. On Dunn and his art, see Robert F. Karolevitz, *Where Your Heart Is: The Story of Harvey Dunn, Artist* (Aberdeen, S.Dak.: North Plains Press, 1970); William H. Holaday III, "Harvey Dunn: Pioneer Painter of the Middle Border" (Ph.D. dissertation, Ohio State University, 1970).

8. Harvey Dunn to H. Dean Stallings, August 29, 1941, reprinted in Holaday, "Harvey Dunn," p. 290.

9. De Smet *News*, June 20, 1930.

10. Aubrey H. Sherwood, *Harvey Dunn, Master Mason* (N.p.:

South Dakota Lodge of Masonic Research, 1964), p. 54; "Harvey Dunn Centennial," *Laura Ingalls Wilder Lore* 10 (Spring–Summer 1984): 7; William Holtz, *The Ghost in the Little House: A Life of Rose Wilder Lane* (Columbia: University of Missouri Press, 1993), p. 280.

11. William T. Anderson, *The Story of the Ingalls* (De Smet, S.Dak.: privately printed, 1971), pp. 30–31.

12. "Harvey Dunn Centennial," *Laura Ingalls Wilder Lore* 10 (Spring–Summer 1984): 7.

13. Karolevitz, *Where Your Heart Is*, pp. 103–7; Aubrey Sherwood, *I Remember Harvey Dunn* (De Smet, S. Dak.: by the author, 1984), p. 4; De Smet *News*, May 25, June 8, August 10, 1950; Sioux Falls *Argus Leader*, August 13, 1950. On Sherwood's efforts to promote Dunn and Wilder in South Dakota, see Dale Blegen, "Aubrey Sherwood of the De Smet News" (Master's thesis, South Dakota State University, 1979), pp. 36–70; Joe Stuart, interview with author, Brookings, October 26, 1992.

14. William Anderson, *Laura Ingalls Wilder; A Biography* (New York: HarperCollins, 1992), pp. 166–67, 196–98, 204–6.

15. Ibid., pp. 208–9; De Smet *News*, June 15, 1939, p. 3.

16. LIW, *The Long Winter* (New York: Harper and Row, 1940), pp. 20–26.

17. On the making of the late-nineteenth-century landscape, see John Fraser Hart, *The Look of the Land* (Englewood Cliffs, N.J.: Prentice-Hall, 1975), and John Brinckerhoff Jackson, *American Space: The Centennial Years, 1865–1876* (New York: Norton, 1972).

18. LIW, *By the Shores of Silver Lake*, pp. 59–60.

19. On the tendency toward exaggeration among western artists, see John Milton, "Plains Landscapes and Changing Visions," *Great Plains Quarterly* 2 (Winter 1982): 57.

20. LIW, *By the Shores of Silver Lake*, pp. 74–75, 158.

21. Ibid., p. 271; LIW, *Little Town on the Prairie*, p. 47; LIW, *These Happy Golden Years* (New York: Harper and Row, 1943), p. 181.

22. LIW, *By the Shores of Silver Lake*, pp. 159, 167; LIW, *The Long Winter*, pp. 56, 266.

23. LIW, *By the Shores of Silver Lake*, p. 66; LIW, *Little Town on the Prairie* (New York: Harper and Row, 1941), pp. 14, 19.

24. LIW, *Little Town on the Prairie*, p. 89.

25. LIW, *The First Four Years* (New York: Harper and Row, 1971), p. 6.

26. Ibid., pp. 18, 23, 45, 49–50, 64.

27. Jon Kalstrom, "Weekly Editor Discusses His Friendship with Harvey Dunn," *South Dakota Magazine* 2 (July 1986): 22.

28. Harvey Dunn, *An Evening in the Classroom* (Tenafly, N.J.: Mario Cooper, 1934), p. 11.

29. C. J. Andres, "Notes on a Lecture of Harvey Dunn," reprinted in Holaday, "Harvey Dunn," p. 232.

30. Saul Tepper, *Harvey Dunn: The Man, the Legend, the School of Painting*, exhibition catalog for the Harvey Dunn School at the Society for Illustrators Museum of American Illustration, June 1–23, 1983, in Dunn File, South Dakota Art Museum, Brookings.

31. Dunn, *An Evening in the Classroom*, p. 13.

32. Karolevitz, *Where Your Heart Is*, pp. 97–101; Aubrey Sherwood, "Harvey Dunn," *South Dakota Conservation Digest* 35 (July–August 1968): 16.

33. Dunn, *An Evening in the Classroom*, p. 24.

34. Ibid.

35. Ibid., p. 36.

36. Harvey Dunn to H. Dean Stallings, August 29, 1941, in Holaday, "Harvey Dunn," p. 289.

37. Quoted in P. K. Thomajan, comp., *I Am My Work, My Work Is Me*, Keepsake no. 9, Friends of the Texas A&M University Library, College Station, Tex., 1980, Dunn File, South Dakota Art Museum.

38. On the romantic tradition in western art, see William H. Goetzmann and William N. Goetzmann, *The West of the Imagination* (New York: Norton, 1986), pp. 42–43, 50, 59, 148–57; William H. Goetzmann and Joseph C. Porter, *The West As Romantic Horizon* (Omaha, Neb.: Center for Western Studies, Joselyn Museum, 1981), pp. 11–30.

39. On prairie madonnas, see Kirsten H. Powell, "Cowboy Knights and Prairie Madonnas: American Illustrations of the Plains and Pre-Raphaelite Art," *Great Plains Quarterly* 5 (Winter 1985): 39–52, and Paul Fees and Sarah E. Boehme, *Frontier America: Art and Treasures of the Old West from the Buffalo Bill Historical Center* (New York: Harry N. Abrams, 1988), pp. 72, 77. On the portrayal of the West as a garden, see Carol Fairbanks, *Prairie Women: Images in American and Canadian Fiction* (New Haven, Conn.: Yale University Press, 1986), pp. 68–71, and Smith, *Virgin Land*, chap. 11.

40. Frederick Jackson Turner, "The Significance of the Frontier in American History," in *Report of the American Historical Association* for 1893, pp. 199–227.

41. On regionalism in American art, see Joseph S. Czesto-

chowski, *John Steuart Curry and Grant Wood: A Portrait of Rural America* (Columbia: University of Missouri Press, 1981); Laurence E. Schmeckebier, *John Steuart Curry's Pageant of America* (New York: American Artists Group, 1943); Wanda M. Corn, *Grant Wood: The Regionalist Vision* (New Haven, Conn.: Yale University Press, 1973); James M. Dennis, *Grant Wood: A Study in American Art and Culture* (New York: Viking, 1975); Henry Adams, *Thomas Hart Benton: An American Original* (New York: Knopf, 1989); Karal Ann Marling, *Tom Benton and His Drawings: A Biographical Essay and a Collection of His Sketches, Studies, and Mural Cartoons* (Columbia: University of Missouri Press, 1985); and Matthew Baigell, *Thomas Hart Benton* (New York: Abrams, 1973).

42. William H. Stott, *Documentary Expression and Thirties America* (New York: Oxford University Press, 1973).

43. Adams, *Thomas Hart Benton*, p. 266. On the mythologizing of the West, see Smith, *Virgin Land*, and Robert G. Athern, *The Mythic West in Twentieth-Century America* (Lawrence: University Press of Kansas, 1986).

44. John Dibbern, "Who Were the Populists? A Study of Grass-Roots Alliancemen in Dakota," *Agricultural History* 56 (October 1982): 677-91; Kenneth E. Hendrickson, Jr., "Some Political Aspects of the Populist Movement in South Dakota," *North Dakota History* 34 (Winter 1967): 77-92; Hendrickson, "The Populist Movement in South Dakota, 1890-1900" (Master's thesis, University of South Dakota, 1959); Terrence J. Lindell, "South Dakota Populism" (Master's thesis, University of Nebraska, 1982).

45. LIW, *The Long Winter*, pp. 302-7; LIW, *These Happy Golden Years*, pp. 64-66; LIW, *Little Town on the Prairie*, pp. 40-46.

46. *State College Farmer and Home Maker* 1: 1 (January 1953): 1; Northwestern Public Service Company, *Annual Report* (1977), in Dunn File, South Dakota Art Museum.

47. The De Smet *Leader*, which began publication in January 1883, was full of ads for and paragraph items about all of the new machinery that was going out to farms in the area. A report from three of the four dealers in town revealed that through August of that year forty-six harvesters and binders, thirty-nine mowers, ninety-three breaking plows, eight threshers, and ten sulky plows had been sold (*Leader*, September 8, 1883). Laura's Pa continued to cut his grain with a cradle, however, rather than go into debt to buy a harvester (LIW, *These Happy Golden Years*, p. 197).

48. Aubrey Sherwood to Joseph Stuart, May 1, 1984, Dunn File, South Dakota Art Museum; Kalstrom, "Weekly Editor Discusses His Friendship with Harvey Dunn," p. 22; Ernest W. Watson, "Harvey Dunn: Milestone in the Tradition of American Illustration," *American Artist* 6 (June 1942): 18; Noel Toberman, interview with the author, Manchester, June 7, 1988.

49. Leo Marx, *The Machine in the Garden: Technology and the Pastoral Ideal in America* (New York: Oxford University Press, 1964).

50. Dunn, *An Evening in the Classroom*, p. 34.

51. Quoted in Thomajan, *I Am My Work, My Work Is Me*.

52. Andres, "Notes on a Lecture of Harvey Dunn," p. 225.

53. Ibid., p. 231.

54. Quoted in John Jellico, "Harvey Dunn, 1884–1952," *Artists of the Rockies and the Golden West* 8 (Fall 1981): 88.

55. LIW and RWL, *A Little House Sampler*, ed. William T. Anderson (Lincoln: University of Nebraska Press, 1988), p. 19.

Index